Watch Your Language

A

STUDENT'S

GUIDE

TO

ENGLISH

Elaine and Peter Robins

Melbourne

OXFORD UNIVERSITY PRESS

OXFORD UNIVERSITY PRESS AUSTRALIA

Oxford New York Toronto
Delhi Bombay Calcutta Madras Karachi
Kuala Lumpur Singapore Hong Kong Tokyo
Nairobi Dar es Salaam Cape Town
Melbourne Auckland Madrid
and associated companies in Berlin Ibadan

OXFORD is a trade mark of Oxford University Press

National Library of Australia
Cataloguing-in-Publication data:

Robins, Elaine.
    Watch your language.

    ISBN 0 19 553430 1.

    1. English literature - Terminology - Juvenile
    literature. 2. English language - Orthography
    and spelling - Juvenile literature. 3. English
    language - Terms and phrases - Juvenile
    literature. I. Robins, Peter. II. Title.

428.1

Illustrated by Terry Denton
Printed by Impact Printing Victoria Pty Ltd
Published by Oxford University Press,
253 Normanby Road, South Melbourne, Australia

Introduction

Many teachers find that the demands and pressures to cover today's English syllabus give few opportunities to help students increase their knowledge of the structure of language and develop the approaches needed for additional insights into the literature they are reading.

It is the recognition of this situation that has prompted us to offer *Watch Your Language* as a resource for teachers and students. It is a reference book for students that provides not only guidance in the formal aspects of writing, but also reinforces the understanding of many literary terms. It covers the main concepts of the English syllabus, so that students may refer to the book whenever they need to. Teachers may direct students to particular points and overcome unnecessary delays in their teaching.

Students need to be encouraged to learn independently and to accept responsibility for clarifying concepts, and teachers will find it advantageous to offer such a support text to which students may refer. Many students are self-motivated and are prepared to challenge and question the language and literary nuances they meet, and these students also need to be catered for. Insights and understandings are seldom gained from a first explanation, and the opportunity to return and reflect is often essential. *Watch Your Language* enables students to fulfil these needs.

A

a / an

These are called indefinite articles.

A is used before words or abbreviations that are pronounced with an initial consonant sound.

> *a* table   *a* UFO   *a* European   *a* bicycle   *a* union
> *a* useless article   *a* photograph

An is used before words or abbreviations that are pronounced with an initial vowel sound.

> *an* egg   *an* honour   *an* aunt   *an* MP   *an* LP record
> *an* unusual happening

abbreviation (from the Latin *brevis,* meaning 'brief')

An **abbreviation** is a shortened form of a word. It may be:

- the first and last letters

> *St*   street, saint
> *Dr*   doctor
> *Mr*   mister

- the first letter, any other letter(s), and the last letter(s)

> *Ave*   avenue
> *Qld*   Queensland
> *Ftle*   Fremantle
> *govt*   government

- the opening letters of a word, followed by a full stop

> *Vic.*   Victoria
> *Tas.*   Tasmania
> *Corp.*   Corporation

- the initial letters

> *RSPCA*   Royal Society for the Prevention of Cruelty to Animals
> *USA*   United States of America
> *ABC*   Australian Broadcasting Corporation.

Some shortened forms have now become accepted words.

> *pram*   perambulator
> *bus*   omnibus
> *phone*   telephone
> *vet*   veterinary surgeon

abstract noun

The **abstract noun** is a noun that indicates a state, feeling or quality.

> a *friendship*
> the *beauty*
> an *opportunity*
> the *excitement*

accept / except

Accept is a verb which means to receive, to take what is offered, and to agree to.

> I *accept* your apology.
> They are pleased to *accept* your invitation.
> She refuses to *accept* your argument.

Except can be:

- a *preposition*

> They all passed the test *except* Bill.

- a *conjunction*, meaning 'unless'

> *Except* when you are on duty, admission is refused.

- a *verb*, meaning to leave out or exclude

> The present company is *excepted* of course.

access / excess

Access can be:

- a *noun*, meaning a way of approach, or gaining entry to

> This road will give us *access* to the camping site.

- a *verb*, meaning to retrieve or store information in a computer

> She needed to *access* the file to gain the necessary information.

Excess can be:

- a *noun*, meaning too much, or an abnormal amount

> His parents showed an *excess* of tolerance towards his misbehaviour that others would never have allowed.

- an *adjective*, meaning more than is necessary, normal or permitted

> The scales indicated an *excess* weight for their luggage, and they had to pay extra.

acronym

An **acronym** is a word formed from the initial letters or syllables of other words.

> *radar*   *r*adio *d*etection *a*nd *r*anging
> *laser*   *l*ight *a*mplification by *s*timulated *e*mission of *r*adiation

scuba	self-contained *underwater* breathing *apparatus*
AIDS	*Acquired Immune Deficiency Syndrome*
QANTAS	Queensland *And* Northern Territory Aerial Services

active / passive voice

These terms are used to classify verbs.

- A verb is in the **active voice** when its subject performs the action.
  The boy (**subject**) *eats* (**active verb**) *the apple* (**direct object**).

- A verb is in the **passive voice** when its subject receives the action.
  The apple (**reversed subject**) *was eaten* (**passive verb**)
  by the boy (**indirect object**).

address (forms of)

The following are the usual forms of address on envelopes and letters
when writing to specific people and places:

	ENVELOPE	SALUTATION
Prime Minister	The Honourable . . . , MP	Dear Prime Minister
Premier	The Honourable . . . , MLA	Dear Premier
Minister (federal)	The Honourable . . . , MP	Dear Minister, or Dear Sir *or* Madam
Minister (state)	The Honourable . . . , MLA Senator the Honourable . . . , MLC	Dear Minister, or Dear Sir *or* Madam
Leader of Opposition	The Honourable . . . , MP	Dear Sir *or* Madam
Member of Legislative Council	The Honourable . . . , MLC	Dear Sir *or* Madam
Member of House of Representatives	Mr *or* Mrs *or* Ms . . . , MP	Dear Sir *or* Madam
Member of Legislative Assembly	Mr *or* Mrs *or* Ms . . . , MLA	Dear Sir *or* Madam

	ENVELOPE	SALUTATION
Senator	Senator . . .	Dear Sir *or* Madam
Governor-General	His *or* Her Excellency . . .	Your Excellency
State Governor	Sir *or* Lady	Your Excellency
Pope	His Holiness Pope . . .	Your Holiness
Archbishop	The Most Rev. and Right Hon. the Lord Archbishop of . . .	Your Grace
Bishop	The Right Rev. Bishop of . . .	My Lord
Clergy	The Rev. . . .	Dear Sir *or* Madam
Knight	Sir A . . . B . . .	Dear Sir A . . .
University	The Vice-Chancellor	Dear Sir *or* Madam
TAFE or School	Principal, Headmaster *or* Headmistress	Dear Sir *or* Madam
Club	The Secretary	Dear Sir *or* Madam
Business company	The Manager	Dear Sir *or* Madam
State libraries	The Director	Dear Sir *or* Madam
Museums	The Director	Dear Sir *or* Madam
Art Galleries	The Director	Dear Sir *or* Madam

addresses (on letters and envelopes)
on letters
- The sender's address is usually placed at the top right-hand corner of a handwritten letter, and it is blocked:

> 2 Custom Street
> FREMANTLE WA 6160

The date usually follows:

> 13 January 1992

- Most businesses use a letterhead which incorporates their address, but personal business letters use a fully blocked style where the address and date are placed at the left-hand margin:

> 2 Custom Street
> FREMANTLE WA 6160

The date is placed two lines beneath the address:

> 3 January 1992

followed by the receiver's address (the addressee):

> The Manager
> Australian Meat-Pie Company
> Lamb Lane
> BULLOCKSVILLE NSW 2999

on envelopes

- The receiver's (or addressee's) address on the envelope is usually placed in the centre of the envelope, blocked, and leaving sufficient room for the stamp.

> Mr R Spring
> 4 Overview Terrace
> NORTH SYDNEY   NSW   2060

- The sender's address should be placed on the outside back flap of the envelope.
- Australia Post recommends no punctuation, no underlining, always include the postcode and write the city and state in capitals.

ad hoc (from the Latin meaning 'for this' [purpose])

The term ***ad hoc*** is used when something is done for a specific purpose and is not a general rule.

> They reached an *ad hoc* decision.
> We made an *ad hoc* arrangement.

adjectival clause (see also **clause**, p. 26)

The **adjectival clause** is a subordinate or dependent clause that is doing the work of an adjective by providing information about a noun or pronoun in the main clause. It is usually introduced by a relative pronoun — WHO, WHOM, WHICH or THAT.

I have the books *which I bought last week.*
(adjectival clause referring to 'books')

The car *that you wanted* has been sold.
(adjectival clause referring to 'car')

The man *whom the police arrested* stole the money.
(adjectival clause referring to 'man')

adjectival phrase

An **adjectival phrase** does the work of an adjective by providing information about and relating to a noun or pronoun in the sentence.

Bradley is a friend *with a keen sense of humour.*
(adjectival phrase relating to 'friend')

I admired the paintings *in the art gallery.*
(adjectival phrase relating to 'paintings')

Weary from the long hike, he staggered to the camp site.
(adjectival phrase relating to 'he')

Note that an adjectival phrase cannot stand on its own as a sentence, but must be linked to a noun or pronoun.

Weary from the long hike, he staggered to the camp site.

adjective

An **adjective** offers information about a noun.

- **Attributive adjectives** come before the noun.

    a *fat* baby
    the *small* hat
    a *dirty* shirt
    happy birthday

- **Predicative adjectives** come after the noun.

    The coat is *wet*.
    The child is *young*.
    They were *lazy*.

adverb

An **adverb** provides information about the verb, adjective, or another adverb in a sentence.

    The boy ran *quickly*.
        (*quickly* gives information about the verb 'ran')
    They had a *really* good time.
        (*really* gives information about the adjective 'good')
    She walks *very* slowly.
        (*very* gives information about the adverb 'slowly')

There are four main kinds of adverbs:

1 *adverbs of manner*, which answer the question HOW?
    carefully   quickly   angrily   noisily

2 *adverbs of time*, which answer the question WHEN?
    tomorrow   now   sometime   soon

3 *adverbs of place*, which answer the question WHERE?
    here   there   somewhere   outside

4 *adverbs of degree*, which answer the question HOW MUCH?
    almost   practically   completely   nearly

Adverbs are frequently formed in English by adding *-ly* to the adjective.

honest	*honestly*
accidental	*accidentally*
beautiful	*beautifully*
slow	*slowly*

Adverbs need to be placed as close as possible to the words that they qualify or provide information about.

    They ran *slowly* down the road.
        (*slowly* gives information about the verb 'ran')

adverbial clause (see also **clause**, p. 26)

The **adverbial clause** is a subordinate or dependent clause that is doing the work of an adverb by giving more information about the verb in the main clause. There are six main kinds of adverbial clauses — TIME, MANNER, RESULT, REASON, CONDITION and PURPOSE.

1 They were delighted *when they heard the news.*
(adverbial clause indicating TIME)

2 He could never forget *however much he tried.*
(adverbial clause indicating MANNER)

3 The drought lasted *so that eventually the rivers were dry.*
(adverbial clause indicating RESULT)

4 Her holiday was spoilt *because her friends were unwell.*
(adverbial clause indicating REASON)

5 You won't succeed *unless you work hard.*
(adverbial clause indicating CONDITION)

6 Lie down *so that the others don't see us.*
(adverbial clause indicating PURPOSE)

adverbial phrase

An **adverbial phrase** does the work of an adverb by indicating TIME, MANNER, RESULT, REASON, CONDITION, and PURPOSE, as these relate to the verb.

1 Rain was expected *during the day.*
(adverbial phrase indicating TIME)

2 You must behave *in a reasonable way.*
(adverbial phrase indicating MANNER)

3 She fell, *receiving a fractured arm.*
(adverbial phrase indicating RESULT)

She fell receiving a fractured arm

4 The boat sank *because of poor navigation*.
> (adverbial phrase indicating REASON)

5 He left *without giving any excuse*.
> (adverbial phrase indicating CONDITION)

6 He worked hard *to achieve success*.
> (adverbial phrase indicating PURPOSE)

Note that an adverbial phrase cannot stand on its own as a sentence, but must be linked to a finite verb.

advice / advise

Advice (pronounced *-ice*) is the noun.
> May I offer you some *advice?*

Advise (pronounced *-ize*) is the verb.
> I *advise* you to accept the offer.

affect / effect

Affect is used principally as a verb that means to influence or to produce a change.
> The story of his adventures *affected* the audience greatly.
> The recession *affects* those who are on low incomes.

Effect may be used as a verb that means to bring about a result.
> The medicine *effected* a remarkable cure.

Effect is more often used as a noun that means a result or consequence.
> There were no side-*effects* from taking the medicine.
> The *effect* of the drought has been hardship for farmers.

affix

Affix is the name given to a *prefix* (see p. 107), or a *suffix* (see p. 143).

agenda (from the Latin *agere*, meaning 'to do or act')

An **agenda** is a list of things to be done or discussed and is often used in this way for the matters to be considered at a meeting.
> The *agenda* for the meeting has been circulated to everyone.

● The plural is *agendas*

The *agendas* are ready for tomorrow.

This is an example of the form an agenda takes:

AGENDA

OPENING REMARKS	Chairperson addresses the meeting
PRESENT	Names of those present recorded
APOLOGIES	Apologies noted from those unable to attend
MINUTES	The record (Minutes) of previous meeting is read and accepted as a correct record.
MATTERS ARISING	Discussion of matters arising from previous Minutes
CORRESPONDENCE	Letters received are tabled and/or discussed
REPORTS	Reports presented by Chairperson, Treasurer and sub-committees
GENERAL BUSINESS	Relevant matters presented and discussed
OTHER BUSINESS	Any other matters for discussion are introduced
NEXT MEETING	Date of next meeting set

---

allegory (from the Greek *allegoria*, meaning 'another speaking')

An **allegory** is a narrative — either in prose or poetry — where details are presented to illustrate a moral, religious, political or social truth. The characters are usually *personifications* of abstract qualities.

Animal Farm by George Orwell and *Lord of the Flies* by William Golding are examples of allegories. In the former, animals portray human qualities and represent political figures. In the latter, the boys' behaviour is a comment on the larger society where dreams of an ideal life disintegrate into brutal savagery.

alliteration

Alliteration is the repetition of the same consonant sound at the beginning of a number of consecutive, or neighbouring words to achieve a particular effect. Alliteration is also an aspect of rhythm and contributes to the overall effectiveness of the piece of writing. Examples are:

> *Pale flakes with fingering stealth come feeling for our faces*
> Wilfred Owen, 'Exposure'

> *Only the stuttering rifles' rapid rattle*
> Wilfred Owen, 'Anthem for Doomed Youth'

allot / a lot

Allot is a verb meaning to assign, to distribute.

> Early settlers *were allotted* land to develop.

A lot is a noun meaning many or much and is always written as two words.

> I can see *a lot* of work ahead of us.

allusion

In a work of literature **allusion** is a brief reference to a famous historical, biblical, classical or literary figure or event. It is used to enrich or enhance a text's meaning and may point up parallels or contrasts.

An example of a **biblical allusion** is to refer to somebody as a *Jonah*, which means a person believed to bring bad luck. (This is based on the Old Testament story of Jonah who, because he would not obey God, brought bad luck to the ship he was travelling on. The sailors threw him overboard and he was swallowed by a whale.)

alter ego (from the Latin *alter*, meaning 'other', and *ego*, meaning 'self')

The term *alter ego* is used to describe a person's *second self*. It is often used to refer to the other side of an individual's personality, different from the one people see.

altogether / all together

Altogether is an adverb meaning completely, wholly or totally.

> Your house is *altogether* different from ours.

All and **together** consist of an adjective *(all)* and an adverb *(together)*.

> The visitors arrived at the house *all together*.
> (*All* [**adjective**] the visitors arrived *together* [**adverb**]).

anachronism (from the Greek *ana*, meaning 'back', and *chronos*, meaning 'time')
Anachronism means a false connection of an event, person or object to a time when that thing was not in existence. Sometimes used as a comic or satiric device by authors to emphasise a point.

There are two well-known examples in Shakespeare's plays *Julius Caeser* and *Antony and Cleopatra*. In the former a clock strikes when these were unknown in Roman times; in the latter Cleopatra suggests a game of billiards when the game did not then exist.

analogy

An **analogy** is a comparison of two things, alike in certain respects, but often dissimilar in essence, and used to provide insight into the nature of one or both.

> When she saw the customers jostling around the sale counter, she was reminded of bees swarming around a honey jar.

He stood before me, beautiful, like a gorilla in a milkshake.

analytical essay

An **analytical essay** is a critical evaluation of a text where the writer looks closely at its structure to note how the ideas have been put together, and the particular ways in which language has been used. The intention is to note what contributes to the overall effect of the piece of writing. The question to be answered often contains key words such as COMPARE, DISCUSS, EXPLAIN and DESCRIBE.

It needs to be remembered that an analytical essay requires not only an evaluation of WHAT is said, but HOW it is said.

anapest

Anapest is a metric foot in poetry that consists of two unstressed syllables followed by a stressed syllable. It is marked as ⌣⌣∕.

⌣ ⌣ ∕
ínterrúpt
⌣ ⌣ ∕
ánalýse
⌣ ⌣ ∕
dísappéar
⌣ ⌣ ∕
súperséde

anecdotal

Anecdotal is an adjective meaning an unsubstantiated claim based on limited personal experience.

anecdote

An **anecdote** is a short personal narrative detailing particulars of an interesting episode or incident in a person's life. It differs from a short story in that it lacks a complicated plot.

antagonist (see also **protagonist**, p. 112)

The **antagonist** is the chief opponent or rival of the *protagonist* in a play or narrative and is used to block the efforts of the chief character to attain his or her goal.

anti-climax

An **anti-climax** occurs when narrative details are arranged in such an order that the lesser, the trivial, or the ludicrous are presented to the reader at a point of mounting intensity and when something greater or more serious is expected.

anti-hero

The **anti-hero** is a *protagonist* (see p. 112) in a narrative or play who lacks the traditional heroic qualities such as physical prowess, or high-minded devotion to duty or to God. While not a villian, the anti-hero is frequently an outsider who passively observes futile aspects of people's lives in twentieth century society. Randall McMurphy in *One Flew Over the Cuckoo's Nest* is an anti-hero.

antonyms

Antonyms are words with opposite meanings.

up	down
good	bad
inside	outside
conflict	harmony
tuneful	discordant

apostrophe (in language)

The **apostrophe** is used in two ways:

- to indicate the omission of a letter or letters in a contraction (see **contraction**, p. 34)
- to indicate possession or ownership (see **possessive apostrophe**, p. 106).

apostrophe (in literature)

In literature an **apostrophe** is a technique of directly addressing an absent person, an abstract concept or quality, or an inanimate object. It is then personified to arrest attention.

> O Rose, thou art sick:
>> William Blake, 'The Sick Rose'

applications (for employment) (see job applications, p. 72)

archetype

The **archetype** is an image, story-pattern, or character type which recurs frequently and evokes strong, often unconscious associations in the reader. Jung, a psychologist, called it the 'collective unconscious' of the human race. He saw it as the blocked-off memory of our racial past, shaped by the repeated experience of our ancestors and expressed in myths, religions, dreams and fantasies.

argumentative essay

The **argumentative essay** presents an argument on a topic which is based on a specific viewpoint. It may offer one, or both sides of an argument, and is often formal and impersonal. The writer's own personal or ideological standpoint is revealed, with recognition of the counter arguments to this. The argumentative essay is usually structured as follows:

INTRODUCTION	refer to topic; offer explanation of argument and possible implications
DEVELOPMENT	introduce points with supporting examples both for and against; state argument clearly; muster support
CONCLUSION	highlight in summary form the points made; draw the threads of the argument together; state position clearly.

articles (see also **a/an**, p. 1, and **the,** p. 148)

These are of two kinds:

- **definite article**: *the* (which is used to indicate a specific object)
  the book   *the* hat

- **indefinite article**: *a* or *an* (which are used to refer to objects more generally)
  a book   *an* apple

aside (in drama)

An **aside** is a brief, scripted comment made by an actor to the audience. It is spoken in an undertone and it is presumed that the words are inaudible to the other actors. Asides are used most frequently in farce and pantomime.

assonance (from the Latin *assonare*, meaning 'sound')

Assonance is the repetition of a vowel sound in near or successive words. Unlike rhyme, only the vowel sounds are the same, not the consonants.

> The students *drowsed* and *drowned*
> In the teacher's *ponderous monotone* -
> Limp bodies looping in the wordy heat,
> Melted and run together, *desks* and *flesh* as one,
> Swooning and swimming in a sea of drone.
> > Colin Thiele, 'Bird in the Classroom'

atmosphere

Atmosphere is the prevailing mood or emotional aura of a literary work which can be created in part by setting or landscape and which helps establish reader expectations as to the course of events.

audience (see also **purpose and audience**, p. 114)

Audience is a term that covers not only those who view a play, but those for whom any fictional or factual work is written.

aural / oral

Aural (from the Latin *auris*, meaning 'ear') means that the communication is based on hearing.

> We had an *aural* test in French where *we listened* to the questions and then ticked what we thought was the correct answer.

Oral (from the Latin *oris*, meaning 'mouth') means that the communication is based on the spoken word.

> For our *oral* test in Italian we had *to tell* the teacher what we saw in the picture.

autobiography (from the Greek *auto*, meaning 'self', *bio*, meaning 'life', *graph*, meaning 'write')

An **autobiography** is the story of a person's life written by him/herself. Autobiographical writing can include *memoirs, diaries, journals* and *letters*.

auxiliary verb (from the Latin *auxilium*, meaning 'help')

An **auxiliary verb** helps or completes another verb. There are three **primary auxiliary verbs:**

- *be* (*am is are was were been*)
- *do* (*does did done*)
- *have* (*has had*)

There are thirteen other auxiliary verbs that are used to express mood or tense:

> *will might ought should can would must could*
> *used (to) may shall can dare*

B

ballad (from the Latin *ballare*, meaning 'to dance')

A **ballad** is a song that tells a story. Ballads have a history of being passed on by word of mouth, often from generation to generation as folk-songs. Thus they have a strong rhyme and rhythm structure that helps people remember the words. They also employ the basic speech rhythms of spoken English, and thus often make use of the *iambic foot*, the light-heavy stress (∪ /) which is the normal speech pattern for many of our sentences. The traditional or literary ballad form became so common that it is often referred to as a ***ballad metre***, which is arranged in four-line stanzas (*quatrains*) with lines 1 and 3 being *iambic tetrameter* and lines 2 and 4 being *iambic trimeter*.

There lived / a wife / at Ush / er's Well. /	4 (*tetrameter*)
And a weal / thy wife / was she; /	3 (*trimeter*)
She had / three stout / and stal / wart sons, /	4 (*tetrameter*)
And sent / them o'er / the sea. /	3 (*trimeter*)

Anonymous, 'The Wife of Usher's Well'

The main characteristics of a ballad are:
- iambic rhythm
- second and fourth line rhyme
- popular subjects are tragedy, death, adventure and the supernatural
- narrative that moves quickly and directly into the story
- use of repetition
- emotions of fear, pity, love, wonder and anger
- suspense and dramatic quality of the narration
- dialogue.

Traditional ballads are narrative folk-songs that may be short but can also have as many as forty stanzas. Some date back to the thirteenth century, but it was not until the eighteenth century that many were written down and copied as they were performed. Many of the finest ballads are Scots or border ballads, where rural life remained undisturbed long after the industrial revolution changed the face of England. Examples of these traditional ballads are 'Sir Patrick Spens', 'Lord Randal' and 'Get Up and Bar the Door'. All these are anonymous.

Allegorical ballads are ballads in which the characters and events are symbolic. An example of this is 'The Rime of the Ancient Mariner' by Samuel Taylor Coleridge.

Australian ballads grew out of the sentiments of the early pioneers and convicts. Ballads about local folk heroes became very popular, especially those that dealt with rebels and outcasts such as Ned Kelly, Moondyne Joe and Captain Starlight. A well-known example is the ballad 'The Wild Colonial Boy'.

'Banjo' Paterson and Henry Lawson wrote ballads that stressed mateship and the spirit of independence. These became known as bush ballads and include 'The Man from Snowy River', 'Waltzing Matilda', 'Casey Jones' and 'The Ballad of the Drover'.

Contemporary folk ballads are popular in many present-day songs such as 'I don't like Mondays' by the Boomtown Rats. Folk singers, such as Woody Guthrie and Bob Dylan, have composed their own ballads and the form continues to be alive and well today.

bathos

Bathos is the effect which is created by dropping from the sublime to the ridiculous — an unintentional anti-climax. It occurs from an unsuccessful attempt to achieve dignity, pathos, or an elevation of style.

between you and me

Between is a preposition and all prepositions in English are followed by the objective case. *I* is the subjective case and cannot be used after **between**. The correct forms are:

> This is *between you and me.*
> I had to decide *between him and her.*
> The argument is *between them and us.*

bias

Bias means looking at something in a one-sided or prejudiced way. Bias is an opinion disguised as fact.

bibliography (from the Greek *biblion*, meaning 'book' and *graph,* meaning 'write')

A **bibliography** is a compilation of the details of texts used in researching a topic. It is alphabetically organised according to author, followed by publication details and set out as follows:

1 author's surname followed by given name or initials or, in the case of anthologies, the editor's name
2 title of text
3 publisher
4 place of publication
5 year of publication

Examples are:

> Drabble, Margaret (ed.), *The Oxford Companion to English*, Oxford University Press, Oxford, 1987.
> Facey, A. B., *A Fortunate Life*, Puffin Books, Ringwood, Vic., 1991.
> Kavanagh, Michael (ed.), *A Swag of Stories*, Oxford University Press, Melbourne, 1987.

biography (from the Greek *bios,* meaning 'life' and *graphie, meaning 'writing')*

A **biography** is a person's life-story written by someone else. The writer may make use of the subject's diaries, letters, photographs, paintings and writings, or draw on personal knowledge and that of others.

The Romans wrote biographies of famous people and Shakespeare drew on some of these for the plots of plays such as *Julius Caesar, Antony and Cleopatra* and *Coriolanus.*

blank verse

Blank verse is unrhymed verse with a regular metre pattern and is not to be confused with **free verse** (p. 58). It applies particularly to unrhymed iambic pentameter. Each line in the poem is accented in this way:

> *and* ONE *and* TWO *and* THREE *and* FOUR *and* FIVE
> But soft! / What light / through yon / der win / dow breaks? /
> It is the East, and Juliet is the sun!
> Arise, fair sun, and kill the envious moon,
> Who is already sick and pale with grief
> That thou her maid art far more fair than she
> Shakespeare, *Romeo and Juliet* (II:ii)

born / borne

These words are sometimes confused. The verb *to bear* has two past participle forms:

born, meaning to give birth to

> Her son was *born* last year.
> She is a *born* leader.

borne, meaning to support, carry, sustain, tolerate, or endure

> She has *borne* a great deal of pain since the accident.
> His story is not *borne* out by facts.
> Ever since their argument he has *borne* a grudge.
> The *airborne* division had gone on manoeuvres.

Bearing a grudge

borrow / lend / loan

Borrow is a verb that means to obtain or receive something from someone on loan with the intention of returning it.

Lend is a verb that means to offer something to someone as a loan with the expectation of getting it back.

Loan is usually used as a noun and it refers to the 'act of lending' or 'the thing that is lent'.

> "I'd like to *borrow* your bicycle from you to go down to the shops."
> "All right, I'll *lend* it to you, but remember it's only a *loan* and I want it back by one o'clock."

Shakespeare offered some wise advice:

> Neither a borrower nor a lender be,
> For loan oft loses both itself and friend.
> *Hamlet* (III:1.47)

bought / brought

Bought comes from the verb *to buy*.

> I *buy* (**present tense**) milk at the local shop, and last week I *bought* (**past tense**) a carton each day.

Brought comes from the verb *to bring*.

> "*Bring* (**present tense**) the washing in, please."
> "I *brought* (**past tense**) it in ten minutes ago."

brackets

Brackets are divided into two main kinds: **round brackets ( )**, called **parentheses** and **square brackets [ ]**, called **brackets.**

Parentheses are placed around words which are not really essential to the main meaning of a sentence, although these words do expand or clarify the meaning. There are no commas before or after the parentheses.

> She managed to take some of her belongings (books, clothing, ornaments, jewellery) with her when she fled the country.

Parentheses are generally used in play scripts for stage directions.

> (*A young Russian officer, in Bulgarian uniform, enters, sword in hand.*)
>
> OFFICER:　　　　*(with soft feline politeness and stiff military carriage)* Good evening, gracious lady. I am sorry to intrude; but there is a Serb hiding on the balcony.
>
> RAINA:　　　　*(petulantly)* Nonsense, sir: you can see that there is no one on the balcony.
>
> 　　　　　　　　　　　　　G. B. Shaw, *Arms and the Man* (I)

Parentheses are used to enclose references and repeated written figures:

> Pollution (see page 12) was the next item discussed.
> Students were required to answer four (4) questions.

Brackets are usually used to indicate additions which are not the original words of the speaker or writer.

> The speaker said that in those days [1850] life in the colonies was very hard.

business letters

Business letters are what the term implies — they conduct business arrangements and are formal and official in their tone. They are direct and to the point. As their style and purpose are different from those of other letters, so are their format and lay-out.

Parts of a business letter:

1 Writer's address (or letterhead)

2 Date (month written in full)

3 Addressee

4 Salutation (various forms):

Dear Sir, Dear Madam, Dear Mr Smith, Dear Ms Jones

5 Paragraphing for main body of letter

6 Complimentary close:

Yours faithfully if *Dear Sir* or *Dear Madam* is used.
Yours sincerely if *Mr Smith* or *Ms Jones* is used.

7 Writer's signature (handwritten name above typed or printed name).

Business letter format — fully blocked style:

SMART & SMART LTD
Address

Date

Mr U R Businessman
1 City Street
CAPITAL CITY STATE 1000

Dear Sir

I am writing to provide you with an example of the fully-blocked letter which is the most commonly used form for business letters today.

As you will note, there are no indentations for paragraphs. Even the Date line (see no. 2 above) and Complimentary close (see no. 6 above) are blocked at the left-hand margin, which allows the typist or word processor to move quickly and easily from line to line and paragraph to paragraph. This amounts to a considerable saving in time and also adds to the appearance and legibility of the correspondence.

The fully-blocked letter has been widely adopted throughout Australia and is used extensively in the Public Service.

Yours faithfully

I. M. Smart

I. M. Smart

C

caesura

A **caesura** is a pause or break in the metrical progress of a line of poetry.

can / may

Can is an auxiliary verb that means to be able to. Its past tense form is *could*.

> I *can* (**present tense**) do much better than that.
> I *could* (**past tense**) have done better than that.

May is an auxiliary verb that means to have permission to. Its past tense form is *might*.

> You *may* (**present tense**) go to the movies tomorrow.
> He *might* (**past tense**) have visited us yesterday.

Usage is making the two words interchangeable, although the distinction is still there. **May** is used on more formal and polite occasions, such as "*May* I help you?".

capital letters

Capital letters are used
- to start a sentence
    > They were leaving.
- for proper names/nouns
    > *Adelaide   Jacqueline*
- for adjectives formed from proper nouns
    > *Australian   English   Italian   Greek*
- for the pronoun
    > *I*
- for days, months, and special holidays
    > *Easter   Christmas   Anzac Day*
- to begin main words in the titles of books, plays, newspapers, poems, and songs
    > *Grapes of Wrath   Death of a Salesman*
- to begin the first word of direct speech
    > He said, "She's late".

- for official titles

   The *Mayor* of *Canning*

- for the Bible, biblical references, deities

   Chapter 5, verses 1-6 *'Then God spoke to him, saying . . .'*

- to begin a line of poetry

   'If you can keep your head when all about you . . .'

catastrophe

The **catastrophe** is the final stage in a tragedy when the *falling action* of a play, which ends the dramatic conflict, leads to the winding up of the plot in the actions that have resulted from the climax.

catharsis

Catharis explains the feeling of pity and fear that an audience feels for the tragic hero which releases, and temporarily resolves, its own emotional tensions. Aristotle used the word to describe the desired effect of tragedy as a 'purgation' of the emotions of pity and fear.

cereal / serial

Cereal is a grain used to produce food. The expression *breakfast cereal* is quite common.

Serial is a story or play produced in several parts. A common expression is *TV serial*.

character

A **character** is created by the author in a literary work. Characters may be *flat*, i.e. built around a single idea or quality, or *rounded*, i.e. complex in temperament and motivation.

Flat characters usually help to convey the action and show how the main character(s) behaves and relates to others. They may establish setting and help to create conflicts. Many flat characters are *stereotypes* (see p. 138).

Round characters are more fully developed and are often the *protagonist* (see p. 112) or *antagonist* (see p. 13) in the story. They are the ones who are more involved in the conflicts, which frequently lead to character change by the conclusion of the story.

characterisation

Characterisation is the technique used by an author in the presentation of characters in a literary work. Characters are revealed by what they say (the *dialogue*), and what they do (the *action*), what they look like (*appearance*), and what others think and say about them (*others*).

Characterisation is achieved in much the same way as we become acquainted with people in real life: we note what they look like; we listen to what they say and how they speak; we observe their gestures, how they move their bodies, and the things they do; and we listen to what other people tell us about them. All of these add to our total understanding of a character.

chauvinism / chauvinist

These terms come from the name Nicholas Chauvin, a legendary Napoleonic soldier who was noted for his vociferous and unthinking patriotism. This is the primary meaning of the words.

More recently, they have been used in a feminist context and the expression *male chauvinist* has become quite popular. This refers to the traditional male belief in his own superiority. It is an unthinking acceptance that one sex is better than the other.

Note: It is incorrect to use **chauvinist** on its own as a synonym for sexist. It should be preceded by *male* or *female*.

choose (rhymes with *news*) **/ chose** (rhymes with *those*)

Choose is the base form of the verb.

> You *choose* which one you want.
> May I *choose* anything?

Chose is the past tense form of *to choose*.

> You *chose* the wrong one.

● The past participle for **choose** is *chosen*.

> I have *chosen* this for you.

cinquain (pronounced *sinkwain*)

Cinquain is a poem of five lines from the French word *cinq*, meaning 'five'. It is arranged as follows:

1 The first line supplies a title.

2 The second line describes the subject.

3 The third line expresses an action.

4 The fourth line expresses a feeling.

5 The fifth line repeats the title, or gives a synonym for it.

Example:

Cloud
Wispy, elusive
Scudding across the sky
Maker of dreams
A cottonwool puff
                    Anonymous

clause

A **clause** is a group of words that contains a subject and a finite verb. Principal kinds are:

- *adjectival*
- *adverbial*
- *conditional*
- *main*
- *noun*
- *relative*
- *subordinate*

Clauses can be *main / independent* or *subordinate / dependent*, and a sentence is composed of one or more clauses.

- The **main / independent clause** can stand on its own as a simple sentence when the rest of the sentence is omitted.
- The **subordinate / dependent clause** cannot stand on its own as a sentence when the rest of the original sentence is omitted.

    The boy took the apple, although he did not eat it.

    The boy took the apple, (**main clause** — can stand on its own as a simple sentence) *although he did not eat it.* (**subordinate clause** — cannot stand on its own as a sentence)

Points to note:

- A sentence must have one or more *main clauses*, which may be joined by linking words such as:

    and but nor or for however nevertheless consequently thus therefore then so yet

- A sentence can have one or more *main clauses* and one or more *subordinate clauses*.

- One or more *subordinate clauses* on their own cannot make a sentence.
- A sentence can have one or more *main clauses* and one or more *subordinate clauses*.
- One or more *subordinate clauses* on their own cannot make a sentence.
- The *subordinate clauses* in a sentence often begin with a relative pronoun (*who, which, that*), or a subordinating conjunction (*if, so, since, while, because, although, that, where, when, until*).

cliché (pronounced *klee-shay*; from the French *clicher*, meaning a sound made by a printing plate)

A **cliché** is an expression or phrase that has been so overused that it has become stale and trite. Examples are:

last, but not least
hit for six
moment of truth
down the track
at this point in time
keep a low profile

Many clichés are *similes* (see p. 130) or *metaphors* (see p. 82).

He charges *like a wounded bull.*
They were *lambs led to the slaughter.*
She's as *cool as a cucumber.*

climax

The **climax** is the most exciting point, or turning point, in the action of a plot. In dramatic structure it refers to the decisive point where the action changes course and begins to resolve itself.

collective noun

The **collective noun** names a collection of many individuals, such as:

army   audience   committee   family   government

- These words are seen as *singular subjects* when the individuals are being referred to as a *collective group.*

The *family* (*it*, **singular**) *is* always quarrelling with its neighbours.
The whole *audience* (*it*, **singular**) *stands* and *cheers* the performance.

- The words are seen as *plural subjects* when *separate individuals* are being referred to:

The *family* (*they*, **plural**) *are* always quarrelling with one another.
The *committee* (*they*, **plural**) *were* unable to agree among themselves.

- When a sentence starts with a singular form, this should be maintained throughout the sentence.

The *team* has started *its* struggle to be the top of *its* division this year.

colloquial

Colloquial language is informal conversational language used in everyday speech. It often includes idiomatic expressions that are characteristic of a particular group or race of people and can be unfamiliar to outsiders. It lies somewhere between slang and standard English.

> That's a *dead cert*.
> He's at a *loose end*.
> She *went crook on/at me*.
> I did it, *fair dinkum*.
> They think he *shot through*.

colon

The **colon** is the punctuation mark **:** and it is used mainly in the same way the equals sign (=) is used in mathematics, indicating that what has gone before is supported by the detail that follows.

> The town has withstood many disasters: floods, earthquakes, typhoons, and the ravages of war.
> Perth: living at its best.
> The items for the meeting were all prepared: tables, chairs, papers, pens, and an overhead projector.

comma

The **comma** is the most frequently used punctuation mark. Its uses are:

- to separate words in a series

NOUNS	Janet bought eggs, cheese, bacon and bread.
VERBS	The lamb jumped, hopped and gamboled.
ADJECTIVES	Mr Brown is kind, generous and helpful.
PHRASES	This is as easy as climbing a mountain, shooting the rapids and swimming the channel.
CLAUSES	It was said that he was lonely, that he kept to himself, and that he had few friends.

- to enclose an elaboration

> The Principal, Mr Brown, was away unwell.

- to act as parentheses

> She said that, no matter what others thought, she would never agree.

common noun

The **common noun** names any one of a class of persons, places, or things.

> *table   house   car   book   game   telephone   radio*

It is not written with a capital letter unless it starts a sentence.

comparative / superlative

These are forms of adjectives and adverbs that are used to express **more** (the **comparative**) or **most** (the **superlative**). They are known as degrees of comparison.

- The **comparative** is used when two things or people are being compared. The **comparative adjective** then takes the suffix *-er*, or is preceded by *more*, while the **comparative adverb** is always preceded by *more*.

POSITIVE ADJECTIVE	COMPARATIVE ADJECTIVE
large	larger
small	smaller
pretty	prettier
beautiful	more beautiful
attractive	more attractive

POSITIVE ADVERBS	COMPARATIVE ADVERBS
quickly	more quickly
greedily	more greedily
easily	more easily
attractively	more attractively

- The **superlative**, or highest degree of comparison, is used when three or more things are compared. The **superlative adjective** then takes the suffix *-est*, or is preceded by *most*, while the **superlative adverb** is always preceded by *most*.

POSITIVE ADJECTIVE	COMPARATIVE ADJECTIVE	SUPERLATIVE ADJECTIVE
large	larger	largest
small	smaller	smallest
pretty	prettier	prettiest
beautiful	more beautiful	most beautiful
attractive	more attractive	most attractive

POSITIVE ADVERB	COMPARATIVE ADVERB	SUPERLATIVE ADVERB
quickly	more quickly	most quickly
greedily	more greedily	most greedily
easily	more easily	most easily

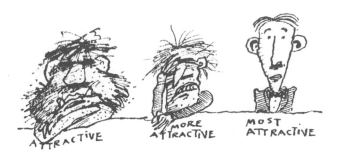

ATTRACTIVE   MORE ATTRACTIVE   MOST ATTRACTIVE

Points to note:
- Some adjectives have irregular comparisons.

good	better	best
bad	worse	worst
little	less	least
much	more	most

- Some adverbs have irregular comparisons.

badly	worse	worst
fast	faster	fastest
well	better	best

- Avoid double comparatives and superlatives.

> She is *cleverer* (not *more cleverer*) than her brother.
> He is the *quickest* (not *most quickest)* courier we've ever had.

- When two adjectives are being compared, *more* is used.

> He is *more stupid* than unintelligent.

- Adjectives of three or more syllables generally use *more / most* to form their comparisons.

> *more / most* difficult
> *more / most* adorable

- Use the *comparative adverb* when it is needed, not the *comparative adjective*.

> Harry learns things *more easily* (not *easier*) than his brother.

- Use the *superlative adjective* when it is needed.

> One of the *most promising* (not *more promising*) of the new athletes is running today.

- In comparisons that indicate less of a quality, the words *less* and *least* are used with all adjectives and adverbs.

Adjective:

intelligent	*less* intelligent	*least* intelligent

Adverb:

carefully	*less* carefully	*least* carefully

compare / contrast

Compare is used to denote similarities between objects.

> He *compared* the two vases and found they matched completely.

Contrast is used when differences are looked for.

> The dry winters in Darwin *contrast* noticeably with its wet summers.

complaint (letters of)

Letters of complaint are set out like business letters. When writing these

- assemble all relevant documents
- detail facts, such as where/when bought/used
- clarify fault/deficiency of goods/service
- enclose photocopied receipts where applicable
- write clearly or type; keep a copy
- paragraph each point made
- keep the letter short and language simple
- be polite in a request for replacement, repair or refund.

complement / compliment

Complement comes from the word 'complete' and means that which completes, adds to, or fills up.

The colour of the curtains *complements* the overall decor of the room.

Compliment means to praise or express regard.

Bill *complimented* the team on its performance.

complex sentence

A **complex sentence** consists of one or more main clauses and one or more subordinate clauses.

When he felt in his pocket (**subordinate clause**) *he found the note* (**main clause**) *which his mother gave him* (**subordinate clause**) *and he passed on the message.* (**main clause**)

Complex sentence = MAIN CLAUSE + SUBORDINATE CLAUSE

complication (in literature)

Complication in literature is that part of a dramatic or narrative plot in which the complication or involvement of affairs starts to develop as a result of the conflicts occurring. The knot is being tied which is to be unravelled later. Complication in drama can be compared to the *rising action,* which can be seen as an **act of complication**.

compound sentence

A **compound sentence** contains two or more main clauses.

> The two boys were late (**main clause**) and the bus should have gone (**main clause**) but it was still waiting. (**main clause**)

The linking word is often *and, but, however, therefore.*

I know it's late, and I said I'd be home at 12.00, and it's now 4 a.m., and 3 days later, but I have had a pretty good time, therefore you are being unreasonable.

compound word

A **compound word** is a word that is formed from joining two or more other words, with or without a hyphen.

> *breakfast bedroom dining-room overhead underground football mother-in-law drop-out*

Note the following plurals of some compound words:

> *brothers-in-law runners-up spoonfuls hangers-on*

conditional clause

A **conditional clause** is an adverbial clause which often begins with the word *if, so, though* or *unless.*

> *If you have that shirt in blue* (**conditional clause**) I shall buy it.
> *Unless you are here on time* (**conditional clause**) we shall start without you.
> *If I were you* (**conditional clause**) I'd take their advice.

All conditional clauses are *subordinate clauses* (see **clause**, pp. 26-7).

conflict (in literature)

Conflict in literature is the struggle between two opposing forces.
There are four basic types:

1 a person in conflict with him/herself
2 a person against another person
3 a person against society
4 a person against nature

Conflict is the basis of all tension and an essential ingredient in narrative and dramatic writing.

conjunction (from the Latin *con,* meaning 'with' and *junct,* meaning 'join')

A **conjunction** joins words, groups of words, or clauses.

She ordered tea *and* cakes.	(words)
He was *but* one of the many losers.	(group of words)
Stop *or* I shall fire.	(clauses)

There are two kinds of conjunctions:

1 **co-ordinating conjunctions** which join words and clauses of the same grammatical type, such as

and   but   yet   or   however   therefore

2 **subordinating conjunctions** which join subordinate clauses to main clauses, such as

because   when   if   though   unless   until

It used to be considered incorrect to begin sentences with the conjunctions *and* or *but.* This is now acceptable practice, provided they are not overused.

connotation (from the Latin *con,* meaning 'with' and *notare,* meaning 'note')

Connotation is an association or idea that is suggested by a word or phrase. A word or phrase may imply more than its literal meaning and the reader or listener may infer a specific response. This is often associated with emotional images, thoughts and feelings.

● The word *friend,* for example, may promote certain reactions, such as *laughter, confidences, parties/outings, sharing/caring.*

Connotations are important in all forms of literature, particularly poetry, which relies very much on conveying images in an economical and effective way.

consonance

Consonance is also referred to as *para-rhyme*, or half-rhyme. The term is used to describe the repetition of only the consonant sounds of words within lines of poetry, for example:

ground   grinned
dazed   dozed

consonant

A **consonant** is any letter of the alphabet that is not one of the five vowels. The letter *y* is a consonant, but it may act as a vowel in words such as:

rhythm hymn synonym sympathy

continual / continuous

Continual means frequently repeated.

His coughing became a *continual* interruption and spoilt the performance for others.

If something is continual, then it is going to stop occasionally. The adverb *continually* implies this too.

Continuous means not stopping until something reaches its conclusion.

The *continuous* noise from the flow of traffic made it impossible for her to sleep.

The adverb *continuously* implies this too.

contraction (see **abbreviation**, p. 1)

A **contraction** is a form of word abbreviation which arises from speech. The most common are those of the verbs *am, are, is, have, has, had, will, shall* and *would*, and the adverb *not* when it is combined with an auxiliary verb. An apostrophe is used to indicate the missing letter(s) and is placed where the letter is omitted.

I'm we're he's you've she's they'd we'll it'll I'd
can't won't shan't aren't didn't isn't don't

Points to note:
- *aren't I?* represents 'am not I?'
- *'d* can stand for either *had* or *would*
- *'s* can stand for either *is* or *has*
- *let's* represents 'let us'
- *won't* represents 'will not'

contrast / compare (see **compare**, p. 30)

convince / persuade

Convince (from the Latin *vincere*, meaning to conquer) is a verb that means a person is made certain of something. Somebody is *convinced of* something, and a *convincing argument* is one that is believed.

Persuade (from the Latin *suadere*, meaning to advise/urge) is a verb that means a person is being urged or encouraged to do something. Somebody is *persuaded to* do something, and a *persuasive argument* is not necessarily one that is believed.

council / counsel

Council is a noun which means a group of people meeting for a discussion or consultation, or an elected group of people appointed to serve in an administrative capacity.

> It was the third time that the *council* had met that week, and there was still no agreement.

A member of a *council* is called a *councillor*.

Counsel can be used as a noun meaning *advice* or *guidance*.

> The doctor's *counsel* was well received and acted on.

It can also be used as a verb meaning *advise* or *guide*.

> The guidance officer *counselled* the students as to their future careers.

The word *counsellor*, meaning *adviser*, comes from *counsel*.

couplet (rhyming) (see also heroic couplet, p. 61)

Rhyming couplet is a verse form of two rhyming lines.

> A troupe of skull-faced witch-men came
> Through the agate doorway in suits of flame,
> Vachel Lindsay, 'The Congo'

crisis (in literature)

Crisis in fiction or drama is the point at which the opposing forces which create the conflict engage in decisive action. It is also the situation in which the *protagonist* (see p. 112) finds him/herself and with which he/she has to deal.

criterion / criteria

Criterion is the singular; **criteria** is the plural.

Criterion takes a singular verb.

> The *criterion* for passing *was* good speech.

Criteria takes a plural verb.

> The proposed *criteria are* much too difficult; we shall have a large number of failures.

currant / current

Currant is a noun that describes a small, seedless dried grape that is used for cooking. *Currant bun/cake* are common expressions.

Current can be an adjective meaning up-to-date, as in *current news/issues*; or it may be used as a noun meaning a steady flow, as in *current of water/air/electricity*.

curriculum vitae (C.V.) / résumé (see job applications, p. 72)

D

dactyl (derived from the Greek for 'finger')

Dactyl is a metrical foot which consists of one stressed syllable
followed by two unstressed syllables.

happiness openly simile interview organise

dash

There are four uses for the dash in written English.

1 in place of a *colon*

He collected all the necessary items for the speaker — table, chair, glass
of water, lectern and overhead light.

2 a *pause* in the flow of words

I'm sure everything will be all right — when he arrives.

3 to indicate an *involuntary break* in a sentence when a speaker is
interrupted

"You're not going to tell me that you — "
"Of course I didn't."

4 in place of *parentheses*

She was dressed ready for the journey — overcoat, boots, gloves and fur
hat — because she had been told how cold it was going to be.

5th use of the dash - defensive

debating

A **debate** is a formal, verbal dispute or argument on a specific topic between two opposing teams of speakers. An adjudicator declares one team to be the winner.

The formal topic is called *the motion*, and it is given either a positive or negative wording, such as:

POSITIVE *that examinations test only those with good memories*
NEGATIVE *that intelligence tests do not indicate an individual's potential to succeed*

The participants are:

- a *chairperson,* similar to a *referee,* who
    introduces speakers and the topic/motion
    rules on interjections
    states the rules and debate procedure
    requests audience questions
    closes the debate.

- a *timekeeper* who
    monitors the length of speeches
    rings a warning bell to indicate the speech is ending
    rings a final bell to indicate the speech must end
    notes the speaker's time.

- an *affirmative team of three speakers* who
    support the motion.

- a *negative team of three speakers* who
    oppose the motion.

The order of speakers is:

    affirmative 1, negative 1, affirmative 2, negative 2, affirmative 3, and negative 3.

The function of each speaker is:

- Affirmative 1
    introduces team
    defines motion from the affirmative viewpoint
    indicates team's line of argument

- Negative 1
    introduces team
    agrees/disagrees with affirmative definition of motion
    redefines the motion if needed, rejecting affirmative viewpoint
    introduces negative arguments, refutes affirmative

- Affirmative 2
    direct rebuttal of negative proposal
    presents affirmative main arguments

- Negative 2
    direct rebuttal of affirmative 2

    presents negative main arguments

- Affirmative 3

    rebuttal of negative arguments
    reinforces own propositions, no new points
    highlights any particular negative points, refutes them
    convinces audience of own arguments
    finishes on positive note supporting motion

- Negative 3

    rebuttal of affirmative arguments
    reinforces own propositions, no new points
    highlights any particular affirmative points, refutes them
    convinces audience of own arguments
    finishes on positive note negating motion.

Points to note:
- speak confidently
- avoid reading notes
- address audience
- gesture if needed
- refer politely to opponents
- avoid talking while others speak
- refrain from abusive interjections
- defer to chairperson
- thank opponents and officials.

demonstrative adjectives

Demonstrative adjectives are called this because they demonstrate or point to a particular noun or nouns. They are: *this, these, that, those.*

> *This* spectator is being a nuisance.
> Pass *these* books to the others, please.
> I'd like *that* apple over there.
> Just put *those* things down, will you?

Points to note:

- A demonstrative adjective is in the singular if the noun is singular.
  > I prefer *that kind* of cake.

- A demonstrative adjective is in the plural if the noun is plural.
  > I prefer *those kinds* of cakes and biscuits.

This applies also to the words *sort* and *type.*

demonstrative pronouns

Demonstrative pronouns are called this because they demonstrate, point to, and identify nouns. They are: *this, that, these, those, one, none.*

> He looked at *these*, decided *that* was the best, and said *none* of the others could match it.
> *Those* are yours; *this* is mine; and he already has *one.*

denotation (see connotation p. 33)

Denotation is the primary meaning of a word, such as its dictionary definition or literal meaning.

> *friend* is defined as 'a person who is closely associated with another and known well'.
> *baby* is 'a very young child, especially one not yet able to walk'.

These are neutral definitions, and offer only the denotation of the word.

denouement (in literature)

This is a French word which means to 'unravel' and refers to the final unravelling of the plot.

dependant / dependent / independent

These words come from the word *depend*.

Dependant is a noun and means a person who depends on another for support, help or aid.

> The parents had four *dependants*: two boys and two girls.

Dependent is an adjective and means that somebody or something depends on another for support.

> When young, children are *dependent* on their parents for everything.

Independent is usually an adjective and means that somebody or something is entirely self-supporting.

> As we grow older, so we become more *independent*, until eventually we can look after ourselves entirely.

descriptive essay

A **descriptive essay** attempts to paint a picture in words of a place, object, people or an event. The writer focuses on the detail of the subject to capture and recreate a particular image.

The intention is to let the reader share the impression in much the same way as a pictorial presentation. Careful consideration is given to style and structure of the writing to ensure that the description is effectively conveyed. Descriptive essays may evoke a particular mood and atmosphere through the use of sensory impressions.

device / devise

Device (pronounced *-ice*) is the noun, and we talk about *the/a device*.

> He saw the new *device* for locating metallic objects lying on the floor of the office.

Devise (pronounced *-ize*) is the verb, and it has a subject.

> The inventor has *devised* a new method for locating metallic objects.

dialogue (from the Greek *dialogos*, meaning 'converse')

Dialogue is the conversation between two or more people as reproduced in writing.

> "What are you doing on Saturday?"
> "Going to the footie, I expect."
> "Can I come with you?"
> "Yeah, don't see why not."

diary

A **diary** is a day-by-day chronicle of events. It is usually a personal, and sometimes intimate, record of events and thoughts kept by an individual. It may also be referred to as a *journal*.

different from / to / than

Different from is the most commonly used form and the one considered the most acceptable. Perhaps that is because the verb *differ* takes the preposition *from*. Things *differ from* one another and are *equal to* one another.

Your house is *different from* mine.

Different to may be used in conversational and informal situations.

Different than is mainly an American expression and is not generally acceptable in formal situations. It is acceptable though when followed immediately by a clause, as in:

Her outlook now is *different than* it was five years ago.

direct / indirect / reported speech

Direct speech means the words that someone says, or said at the time of an event. They are enclosed in speech or quotation marks, which are called *inverted commas*.

"I think we ought to leave at seven," said Bill.

Indirect (reported) speech means the words that someone said which are written down (reported) after the event. No inverted commas are used.

Bill said that he thought we ought to leave at seven.

discreet / discrete

These are easily confused adjectives.

Discreet means keeping confidences and secrets, being cautious and tactful, and thus avoiding embarrassment.

> We can trust him; I know he will be *discreet*.

> She was asked to be *discreet* and to keep the information to herself.

Discrete means separate, distinct, or unconnected.

> You should finish with a series of *discrete,* random numbers.

disinterested / uninterested (see **uninterested**, p. 155)

documentaries (film)

Documentaries are scripted presentations of an important topic or issue, usually of a serious nature. They are like non-fiction films that deal with real-life situations, and record people, places and events. Some topics chosen for documentaries are nature/wildlife, drug abuse, land rights, nuclear radiation, surfing, aspects of war, well-known people, and so on.

A documentary could be described as a *creative interpretation of reality*. Objectivity or neutrality is not always apparent in documentary films. They are subject to the directors' *selection* of images and information. Music and light, editing, camera angles, script, etc. can all be used to CREATE a particular version of reality, i.e. the author's/director's point of view is the interpretation of events being offered to the viewer.

The questions we need to pose when viewing documentaries are:
- What aspects of the main topic are being considered?
- What is the source of the information?
- Does the information have a balanced presentation?
- Does the film footage generate the commentary, or has the point of view come first and the film been used to confirm it?
- Are the people interviewed biased in their contributions?
- What values and attitudes are being reinforced?

We also need to pose questions about how the camera has been used to construct the documentary, remembering that it gives a powerful point of view to any televised event:
- How are the camera angles chosen and how are people and objects positioned?
- What expressions are captured on people's faces?
- How are varying shots (from close-ups to long shots) used?

drafting (see **writing process**, p. 163)

drama

A **drama** is a story told by means of characters speaking *dialogue* (see p. 41). Aristotle called it 'imitated human action'. It is a literary composition where actors take the roles of the characters and enact the script, usually in a theatre. Writers of drama are called *playwrights*.

DRAMA STUDY PRO FORMA

Ask these questions when reading a play:

Exposition (see p. 52)
- How does the visual effect of stage setting (scenery, props, lighting) contribute to the overall atmosphere?
- Does the stage setting indicate some particular time or period?
- Are there any musical or sound effects that are significant to the opening?
- Do the characters form part of the overall setting or atmosphere?
- Are their costumes significant?
- What background information is given and how is this provided?
- What do we learn about the characters and their relationships?
- How are possible conflicts foreshadowed?

Development
- Is the language formal, informal, colloquial, or crude? Why?
- Is there a contrast of language styles between the characters?
- How do the characters and their actions shape the events?
- What new characters are introduced and how do they develop the action?
- In which scene or act does the climax occur?
- How does this affect the characters?
- What thematic interpretation can be made from the events?
- How are the conflicts resolved?
- Is the title significant?

dramatic irony

Dramatic irony exists when a character in a literary or dramatic work perceives a situation in a limited way while the reader or audience is aware of a greater significance. The irony is in the contrast between the meaning intended by the speaker and the added significance seen by others.

dramatic monologue

Dramatic monologue is a one-sided conversation presented in a lyric poem where a speaker addresses him/herself to one or more persons who are present but do not reply. Dramatic monologue has three characteristics:

- it presents a dramatic moment in the life of the speaker
- it reveals his/her character
- it includes a listener who does not speak but who affects the development of the monologue.

The poet Robert Browning (1806-61) is famous for his development and mastery of the dramatic monologue. Chaucer had used some of its techniques in 'The Wife of Bath's Prologue' and Tennyson had used it in his poem 'Ulysses', as well as several other poems. It is still a popular form of poetry.

Dramatic monologue can also be used as a narrative technique in prose fiction.

E

each / every

Both words are singular, as are:

anyone anybody either everybody neither nobody somebody

When they are subjects, then the verbs should be in the singular also.

Each of you *is* required to sign the visitor's book.
Neither is appropriate dress for this occasion.

editing (see writing process, p. 163)

editorial

An **editorial** is an article in a newspaper where the writer comments on an issue and expresses a point of view, which is usually in line with the newspaper's *editorial policy*. It does not convey information, but rather expresses a subjective view about some item of news.

effect / affect (see affect, p. 9)

e.g. / for example (from the Latin *exempli,* meaning 'example' and *gratia,* meaning 'favour')

This term is used to introduce an example and is usually preceded by a comma (or parentheses). A comma is not usually used after it.

Many countries in Asia, *e.g.* India, Indonesia, Malaysia and Singapore, were once controlled by European countries.

either / neither (pronounced like *tree* or *try*)

These mean *either one / neither one* and are singular. They should be followed by the singular verb.

> *Either* of the boys *is* suitable for the vacancy.
> *Neither* visitor *was staying* for the entertainment.

either / or and **neither / nor**

Either is followed by **or**; **neither** is followed by **nor**.

If two subjects are joined by these correlatives, then the verb should agree with the subject that comes after *or* and *nor*. This occurs because the first clause introduced by *either/neither* is never completed; the second clause introduced by *or/nor* is always completed.

> *Either you* (are going to win) (**first clause incomplete**) *or I am going to win.* (**second clause complete**)
> *Either they* (are wrong) (**first clause incomplete**) *or he is wrong.* (**second clause complete**)
> *Neither he* (was present) (**first clause incomplete**) *nor his friends were present.* (**second clause complete**)
> *Neither her parents* (were there) (**first clause incomplete**) *nor she was there.* (**second clause complete**)

Either / or and **neither / nor** should be placed so that each part of the correlative controls the same part of speech. The sentence is then balanced.

> Shut *either* the window *or* the door.　　(*window/door* = nouns)
> *Neither* visit *nor* speak to them.　　(*visit/speak* = verbs)
> He is *either* stupid *or* lazy.　　(*stupid/lazy* = adjectives)

elegy

An **elegy** is a lyric poem composed to mourn the death of someone in a solemn, formal manner, or to commemorate some past event. The usual tone is one of sadness or melancholy. No special metre or stanza-form is required, although some simple form, such as a ballad, is often preferred. Examples are Gray's 'Elegy Written in a Country Churchyard' and Tennyson's 'Break, Break, Break'.

Elizabethan sonnet (see **sonnet**, p. 130)

emigrant / immigrant / migrant (from the Latin *migrare*, meaning 'to leave/depart/to live elsewhere')

- An **emigrant** is someone who leaves a country to live elsewhere. The prefix 'e' means *from*.

- An **immigrant** is someone who comes into a country to live. The prefix 'im' means *into*.

  Thus people who leave one country to live in another are both **emigrants** from their original country, and **immigrants** in their new country.

  The new *immigrant* to Australia was an *emigrant* from Britain.

- **Emigrant** and **immigrant** give the words *emigration* and *immigration*.

- **Migrant** is an Australian term for a recent *immigrant*.

  They were living in a hostel for *migrants* in Adelaide.

Its general meaning is a person or animal that moves from one place to another.

emotive writing

Emotive writing aims to work on the reader's emotions so that feelings such as joy, sorrow, anger or indignation are aroused. Its intention often is to bring about a change or to reinforce attitudes, opinions or behaviour. The main approaches used are often *description, narration* and *humour*. The expression 'colourful language' is used to describe the style of emotive writing.

end rhyme (in poetry)

End rhyme is the repetition of the sound(s) at the end of a line of verse in subsequent lines.

> Under a spreading mulberry tree
> The local burglar *lies;*
> He is a strong and hairy man,
> With whiskers round his *eyes;*
> And the muscles of his brawny arms
> Keep off the pesky *flies.*
>
>   Anonymous

end stopped (in poetry)

This term is applied to a line of verse where the sense and the metre coincide in a pause at the end of the line. Rhyming couplets often synchronise in this way.

> I am a young executive. No cuffs than mine are cleaner;
> I have a Slimline brief-case and I use the firm's Cortina.
> In every roadside hostelry, from here to Burgess Hill,
> The *maitres d'hotel* know me well and let me sign the bill.
>
>   John Betjeman, 'Executive'

enjambement / enjambment (from the French meaning 'to straddle')

Enjambement is used to describe the running on of the sense and grammatical structure of one line of verse into the next.

> That's my last Duchess painted on the wall,
> Looking as if she were alive. I call
> That piece a wonder, now: Fra Pandolf's hands
> Worked busily a day, and there she stands.
>
>   Browning, 'My Last Duchess'

enquiry / inquiry

Enquiry is generally used for requesting information on a topic.

> The large departmental store had an *enquiry* counter for its customers.
> She *was enquiring* about the health of her friend.

Inquiry is generally used to indicate that an investigation is under way or that research is being conducted on a topic.

> They are calling for a public *inquiry* into the disaster.
> The police *are inquiring* into the events.

envelop / envelope

Envelop is a verb meaning to surround or to cover. It is pronounced en-*vel*-op, with the stress on the second syllable.

Envelope is a noun meaning the paper covering made for a letter. It is pronounced either *en*-vel-ope or *on*-vel-ope, with the stress on the first syllable.

epic

An **epic** is a long narrative poem, originally handed down in the oral tradition. It presents characters of high position, such as kings, warriors and folk heroes, in a series of adventures which form a whole, and is written in an *elevated style*. Homer's *Odyssey* is an example of an early epic, in which the adventures of Odysseus are recounted as he returned from the Trojan wars to his island home in Ithaca.

epigram

An **epigram** is a short, witty poem or comment which expresses concisely a memorable thought or idea. Originally it meant an inscription on a monument or statue. An example is:

> Some people eat to live
> While others live to eat.
> Anonymous

epitaph

An **epitaph** is an inscription or message on a tombstone, written to commemorate someone's death.

> Here lies our Sovereign Lord the King,
> Whose word no man relies on,
> Who never said a foolish thing,
> Nor ever did a wise one.
> Rochester, 'Charles II'

essay

An **essay** is a number of linked paragraphs based on a topic. The principal kinds of essays are: *analytical, argumentative, descriptive, expository, reflective.* (See also separate listings for each of these.)

et al. (from the Latin *et alii*, meaning 'and other people')

This term is used for referring to a book or article written by a number of people when only the first contributor is mentioned.

> Stone, James, et al., *Management in Australia*, Prentice-Hall, Sydney, 1985.

etc. (from the Latin *et cetera*, meaning 'and other things', pronounced *etsetera*)
The term should not be used to refer to people. It is used mainly in technical or informal writing and should not be used in formal writing such as essays. Since *et* means 'and', it is incorrect to write *and etc.*

eulogy

A **eulogy** is a formal, dignified speech or piece of writing which praises a person or thing.

euphemism (from the Greek *eu*, meaning 'pleasant' and *pheme*, meaning 'speech')
Euphemism means using a pleasant form of words to describe something less pleasant. While there may be occasions when euphemisms are acceptable, they are usually employed to hide or obscure facts in order to present or create a false picture.

> *put to sleep* (kill)
> *friendly fire* (kill own troops)
> *cosmetic deficiency* (ugly)
> *terminal episode* (death)
> *terminological inexactitude* (lie)
> *gone to heaven* (died)

every / each (see **each**, p. 46)

except / accept (see **accept** p. 2)

excess / access (see **access** p. 2)

exclamation mark

This is sometimes referred to as a *startler*, which is an apt name for its function. Its main uses are:

- to indicate strong feelings or urgency
     Help! Wait! Stop that! Keep quiet!
- to emphasise oaths and loud noises
     Damn! Blast! Hell's bells! Crash! Wham! Woosh!
- to show that words are being used in a special way
     You must be joking! And you said it was all right!
- to complete an interjection after the words *how/what*
     How beautiful that is! What fun we're having!

Points to note:
- NEVER overuse exclamation marks.
- NEVER double or treble exclamation marks.

exposition (in literature)

Exposition in literature is the introduction in a novel to the writer's plot where details are being exposed or revealed to the reader. The writer offers clues about who is in the story and their involvement with one another, as well as hints to possible conflicts and what may develop. The exposition is the writer's way of engaging the reader, promising interest and involvement, suspense and excitement.

expository essay

An **expository essay** sets out to *expose* the topic as seen through the eyes of the writer, who describes what happened and explains the reactions to a situation. It is mainly a reliving of an experience, presented in a narrative framework. Only one viewpoint is usually offered.

expressive writing

Expressive writing is used to form opinions, develop attitudes and shape beliefs. It is used to analyse experience and give free expression to thoughts and feelings that accompany experiences. It is the centre point from which other language forms develop.

F

fable

A **fable** is a brief story, usually with animal characters, that points clearly to a moral or lesson. It emphasises a certain kind of behaviour which is often selfish or unkind, and indicates weaknesses. The most well-known fables are those written by a Greek called Aesop some 2500 years ago. He wrote such fables as 'The Hare and the Tortoise' and 'The Lion and the Mouse'.

facsimile / fax (from the Latin *fac simile*, meaning 'make something like it').

A **facsimile** is an exact copy or reproduction. The modern form is the process of transmitting a written, printed or pictorial document telegraphically. The document is scanned photoelectrically and can be transmitted rapidly to another receiver anywhere in the world.

fact / opinion

Fact is something that everyone agrees to, and that can be proved and demonstrated. Characteristics of a factual or *objective* style of writing are:

- aims to give facts
- clear and concise wording
- covers all aspects
- quotes comments and sources

Opinion is a particular viewpoint adopted by the transmitter, and is subjectively influenced by personal interests and emotions. Characteristics of an opinionative or *subjective* style of writing are:

- offers writer's own views
- attempts to influence
- proposes suggestions and indications as to outcomes

factual / formal / functional writing

Factual, formal and **functional writing** deal with topics in a mainly impersonal and objective way. It offers the reader information in the expected form, such as reports, instructions, surveys, reviews and directions. The writer's personality does not intrude as the intention is to report the facts as objectively as possible. It is an intellectual response to the topic, not an emotional one.

farce

A **farce** is a type of comedy which depends for its effect on *outlandish situations* rather than on witty dialogue, plot or character. The humour arises from gross incongruities, coarse wit or horseplay. The characters are often stereotypes and stock figures. The plays of the French playwright Moliére have a strong farcical component.

Many present-day TV situation comedies have exaggerated characters, and rely on clowning and slapstick, for example the shows of Lucille Ball and the series 'All Together Now'.

fax (see **facsimile**, p. 53)

feature article

A **feature article** is an imaginative piece of writing that aims to provide background and add interest to current news stories, or to explore and comment on issues of interest. The main types of feature articles are:
- personality profiles
- human interest stories
- trends and fashions
- in-depth investigative stories
- background to current issues
- reviews of plays, films, television, books and concerts

Feature articles aim to *inform, entertain, persuade* and *emotionally involve* the reader. Conventions of these are:
- illustrations and eye-catching headline
- opening paragraph which captures the reader's attention
- short paragraphs and column format
- colourful, imaginative and simple language
- sub-headings

Many newspapers contain regular and special feature articles as well as a weekly magazine supplement that consists exclusively of features.

fewer / less

Fewer is the comparative of *few* and means a smaller number of. It should be used when plural nouns are being referred to, particularly when these can be counted. **Fewer** is used to indicate number.

> We have *fewer* people living in our house this week.
> We asked the milkman to leave *fewer* cartons of milk.

Less is the comparative of *little* and means a smaller amount or quantity of. It should be used with singular nouns that refer to mass or quantity.

> There is *less* noise in our house with people away.
> We are needing *less* milk, butter and bread.

Remember: **Fewer** for *number* and **less** for *quantity*.

fiction

Fiction is narrative writing that is developed from the writer's imagination rather than from history or fact. The term is most frequently associated with novels, short stories and plays. But a writer may exploit factual information to stimulate his or her imagination as in *historical romance fiction* and *science fiction*. The main function of fiction is to entertain and interest the reader, but it may also instruct and persuade.

figurative language

Figurative language is the effect caused by using language in a fresh and original way by departing from the normal order, construction and literal meaning of words. It usually embodies various *figures of speech* such as simile, metaphor, personification, hyperbole, and so on.

figures of speech

These are literary devices used to create clear and forceful imagery. The most common are:
- *simile*
- *metaphor*
- *personification*
- *alliteration*
- *onomatopoeia*
- *assonance*
- *consonance*
- *hyperbole*
- *irony*

(See also separate listings for each of these.)

finite verb

The **finite verb** is a verb that
- has a subject
- changes according to the person or number of that subject
- expresses a tense.

> The bus *stops*.
> The bus *is stopping*.
> The bus *has stopped*.
> (Singular subject *bus,* with the verb changing tense)
> The buses *stop*.
> The buses *are stopping*.
> The buses *have stopped*.
> (Plural subject *buses*, with the verb changing tense)

first person p.o.v. (see **point of view**, p. 104)

flashback

This is a technique sometimes used by writers which varies the chronological order of the narrative. The story usually begins at, or near, a climax, then goes back in time to trace past events.

foot-metrical (in poetry)

This term refers to the unit of rhythm in a poem. It usually consists of one stressed or long syllable and one or more unstressed or short syllables. The main kinds are:

- iambic foot

    delight

- trochaic foot

    gather

- anapestic foot

    disappear

- dactylic foot

    happiness

- spondee foot

    heart break

(See also separate listings for each of these.)

forms of address (see **address**, p. 3)

free verse

Free verse is poetry that does not contain any set or regular rhyme scheme or metrical pattern. If stanzas occur they may be of random size with irregular line length.

> A snake came to my water-trough,
> On a hot, hot day, and I in pyjamas for the heat,
> To drink there.
>
> In the deep, strange-scented shade of the great dark
>   carob-tree
> I came down the steps with my pitcher
> And must wait, must stand and wait, for there he was
>   at the trough before me.
>
> D. H. Lawrence,' Snake'

Note: **Free verse** is not to be confused with the regular rhythm and pattern of *blank verse* (see p. 19).

full stop

The **full stop** is used mainly

- to indicate where a sentence ends that is neither a direct question nor an exclamation
- to indicate an abbreviation
- for decimal fractions, times and dates.

future tense

The **future tense** is one of the three main tenses of a verb: *past, present* and *future.*

Simple future tense is formed by adding *shall* or *will* to the verb.

> I *shall see* you there.
> They *will see* you there.

Continuous future tense is formed by adding *shall be* or *will be* to the present participle of the verb.

> I *shall be seeing* you.
> They *will be seeing* you.

Perfect future tense is formed by adding *shall have* or *will have* to the past participle of the verb.

> I *shall have seen* you.
> They *will have seen* you.

G

gender

Gender in English grammar is indicated by the use of the pronouns *he,*
she or *it* to indicate the sex of the subject. These become *him, her* and *it*
when the object.

Gender is also used to indicate the difference between being male
and being female and is the product of a society's culture. Males and
females are allocated specific rôles, behaviours and social expectations.
These are frequently stereotypical and reinforced by print and
non-print texts. **Sex** is *biologically determined* while **gender** is *culturally
constructed*.

genre

Genre is a term which signifies a specific literary form, such as poetry, short story, novel or drama. However the term can also be applied within each of these categories to indicate other classifications, such as romance, science fiction, adventure and so on. Such stories can be grouped together because of their content and the pattern of presentation that they follow.

Genres have developed because writers in a particular society have needed to express their thoughts and feelings, or to reflect on the influences at work in that society. The pioneering of the west in America, for example, promoted the 'Western' as a genre, while the introduction of modern police methods and detection led to the mystery thriller.

gerund / noun verbal

The **gerund** is the *-ing* form of the verb being used as a *noun*.

Winning gave him much pleasure.   (noun = subject)
I remember *winning* here before.   (noun = object)

- Errors arise when a possessive is introduced which relates to the gerund. Since it is a noun, the possessive forms *my, your, his, her, its, our, their* should be used.

  His winning gave us much pleasure.   (Not *him winning*)
  I remember *our winning* here before.   (Not *us winning*)

- When a proper noun is used with the gerund, then this should end with a possessive apostrophe.

  Jan's winning gave us much pleasure.   (Not *Jan winning*)
  I remember *Matt's winning* here before.   (Not *Matt winning*)

The distinction becomes clear in the sentences:

I watched *Kate running*.   (I watched *Kate when she was running*.)
I watched *Kate's running*.   (I watched *the running of Kate*.)

In the first sentence Kate (noun) is being watched, while in the second sentence it is Kate's running (noun) that is being watched.

grammar

Grammar is an attempt to describe the features of a language and to note the structures used in spoken and written forms. These then become the acceptable rules, and these are followed by the transmitter and receiver which enable a communication to take place.

haiku

Haiku is a Japanese poetry form in which a particular emotion or image is compressed into seventeen syllables in three lines. Lines 1 and 3 have five syllables and line 2 has seven.

> Leaf hangs on the tree　　　　　　(5)
> Turning old and brown and green　(7)
> Until the wind blows.　　　　　　(5)
>
> Anonymous

hero / heroine

The **hero** is the central character (male or female) in a fictional work. As the term is synonymous with a person of noble qualities, *protagonist* (see p. 112) is more commonly used.

The word **heroine** is gradually being replaced by **hero** to avoid sexist connotations.

heroic couplet (see also **couplet**, p. 36)

In poetry this consists of two consecutive rhyming lines of *iambic pentameter* which encapsulate a complete thought or idea. Chaucer established and developed the use of this verse form, and later the poets Dryden and Pope made it their own.

> All human things are subject to decay
> And, when fate summons, monarchs must obey.
>
> Dryden, 'Mac Flenkoe'

homophone (from the Greek *homo,* meaning 'same' and *phone,* meaning 'sound')

Homophone is the name given to words that have the same sound but differ in meaning and spelling. Examples are:

bare/bear
allowed/aloud
know/no
cereal/serial

however

However can be used as:

1 an adverb, when it means 'in whatever way', 'no matter how'.

However (in whatever way) you managed to wreck the car, I shall never understand.

Mary always does her best *however* (no matter how) difficult she finds the task.

Points to note:

- There is no comma after **however.**
- It can start a sentence.
- As an adverb, it can qualify an adjective or a verb.

2 A co-ordinating conjunction or connective, when it means 'but' or 'nevertheless'.

I want you to finish the job; *however* (but), you can take as long as you like.

Jane has worked well this year; *however* (nevertheless), she will have to make an even greater effort in Year 12.

Points to note:

- **However** is preceded by a semi-colon.
- It is followed by a comma.
- It joins two main clauses.
- The semi-colon could be replaced by a full-stop and two separate sentences formed.

Important: It is incorrect to use a comma before **however** when it is acting as a connective, meaning 'but', and is linking two main clauses.

INCORRECT   The girls are late, however they probably have a good excuse.
CORRECT   The girls are late; however, they probably have a good excuse.

3 an adverb in parenthesis where it means 'nevertheless'.

>He does not, *however*, like to go camping.

>*However*, if Anne tries hard, she will succeed.

Points to note:

When **however** is used parenthetically

- it has commas before and after it
- it can open a sentence, and is then followed by a comma
- it is used as a means of contrast and emphasis.

hubris (from the Greek *hubris,* meaning 'wanton insolence')

Hubris is overweening pride which results in the misfortune of the *protagonist* (see p. 112) in a tragedy. The character displays excessive pride, ambition and over-confidence which lead him or her to break or ignore a divine warning, and so cause his or her downfall. Examples:

- Oedipus ignores the gods and suffers the consequences.
- Macbeth's overriding ambition leads to his downfall.

hyperbole

Hyperbole is the technique of deliberate exaggeration which is used for expressive or comic effect. Specific examples often become everyday expressions.

>I've told you that *thousands of times.*

>He's had *hundreds* of teeth out.

>Her sponge cakes are so light they *float above the table.*

hyphens

Hyphens are used more as marks of spelling and pronunciation than as punctuation. They indicate that

- two or more words belong together

  sister-in-law
  non-stick
  band-aid
  twenty-three

- two parts of a word belong together when broken at the end of a line

  be-lieve
  dis-appear
  stop-ping
  fac-tory
  contra-dict

This breaking of words is known as *syllabification*. Each part can be pronounced as it would sound in the whole word.

physiology *physi-ology*   physiological *physio-logical*

Points to remember:

- Put the hyphen at the end of the line, not at the beginning of the next line.
- Separate the word at the end of a syllable and nowhere else.
- Words of one syllable cannot be hyphenated.
- Never leave one letter of a word at the end of a line.
- Avoid hyphenating names of people and places.

I

I / me

I is the *subject* form of the pronoun, and it is courteous to place it second in such sentences as:

> You and *I* will visit them.
> My sister and *I* can see him.
> Your friend and *I* borrowed the car.

Me is the *objective* form of *I* and needs to be used in such expressions as:

> They saw *me* at the football.
> He invited you and *me* to the party.
> These presents are for *me* and him.
> This is between you and *me*.

iambic foot (in poetry)

Iambic foot consists of an unstressed and stressed foot, written ∪ /.

> invént revíew depárt appóint alóne

The iambic foot is the basic speech rhythm of spoken English and many poems exploit the light-heavy stress pattern. It is the way in which sentences often begin in ordinary speech.

idiom

Idiom is a peculiarity of expression with a particular grammatical or syntactical construction which cannot be translated literally into another language. All languages contain such idiomatic expressions which tend to confuse foreigners. Examples are:

> It's your shout.
> Bring a plate.

i.e. (from the Latin *id est,* meaning 'that is'.)

This abbreviation is used for clarifying and emphasising what has gone before, and is usually preceded by a comma. Normally a comma is not needed after it.

> They noted that most medals were won by the largest sporting nation taking part, *i.e.* the United States of America.

imagery

Imagery refers to the *collection of images* within a literary work and are the sensory details which tend to evoke in the reader emotional suggestions which offer the mental pictures. In some literary works particular images form patterns by their repetition.

imperative mood (see also **mood (in verbs)**, p. 84)

This is a verb form used to express a command or order.

> *Shut* the door!
> *Be* careful!
> *Mind* your head!
> *Stop*!

imply / infer

Imply means to hint, suggest or insinuate. It is what a speaker, writer or performer does, so only the *transmitter* of a communication can *imply*.

> The principal *implied* that the culprits would be punished.
> Her body language *was implying* total disagreement.

The Principal implied that the culprits would be punished !!

Infer means to draw a conclusion, deduce. It is what a listener, reader or observer does, so only the *receiver* of a communication can *infer*.

> By his grin, we *inferred* that he was happy with the result.
> His comments led me *to infer* that there would be problems.

Points to note:
- **Imply** gives the noun *implication*.
- **Infer** gives *inference*.

indefinite article (see **a/an**, p. 1)

indefinite comparative

The **indefinite comparative** is an unclear comparative in that the two items being compared are not identified. Advertisements exploit indefinite comparatives when using such expressions as

> washes *whiter*
> keeps *cleaner*
> lasts *longer*

This leads to the question: *whiter, cleaner, longer* than what?

indicative mood

This is a verb form that states a fact or asks a question.

> He *crashed* his new car last week.
> *Would* you *tolerate* such irresponsibility?
> It *is* a fine day for a trip to Rottnest.

indirect object

The **indirect object** refers to a noun or pronoun that indicates who or what is linked to the *direct object* of the verb.

The indirect object can be understood by asking *to (?)* or *for (?)*, if these are not already in the sentence.

> *He wrote James a letter.*
> > He wrote a letter (**direct object**) to James (**indirect object**).
> *We gave the dog a new collar.*
> > We gave a new collar (**direct object**) to the dog (**indirect object**).
> *She bought me a present.*
> > She bought a present (**direct object**) for me (**indirect object**).
> *Save us one.*
> > Save one (**direct object**) for us (**indirect object**).

indirect / reported speech

This is the reporting of the words that a speaker used.

> *'I've lost my hat,' said Jane.* (**direct speech**)

becomes

> *Jane said that she had lost her hat.* (**indirect speech**)

Note that in indirect speech
- *I* becomes *she*
- *lost* becomes *had lost*
- there are no speech marks
- *that* is used to introduce the reported words.

"Do you know what has happened?" asked Michael. (direct speech)

becomes

Michael asked if we knew what had happened. (indirect speech)

Note that in indirect speech

- *you* becomes *we*
- *know becomes knew*
- *has* become *had*
- there are no speech marks or question marks
- *if* is used to introduce the reported words.

infinitive

The **infinitive** is the verb form that is generally introduced by *to*.

> He wants *to go* there on Saturday.
> They came *to see* him in hospital.
> *To find* work is not an easy matter.

Some auxiliary verbs take an infinitive without *to*.

> She can *visit* us whenever she likes.
> We must *decide* what accommodation we require.
> They said that I should *go* and see the doctor.

The infinitive may be:

• present tense	*to walk*
• past tense	*to have walked*
• present continuous	*to be walking*
• past continuous	*to have been walking*

info-tainment

Info-tainment is a recent hybrid word formed from **info**(rmation) and (enter)**tainment**. It relates particularly to commercial television news broadcasts that offer a mix of glitzy advertising campaigns, catchy jingles and current affairs items to woo viewers to tune in early and stay tuned to that particular channel. News is becoming like fictional drama and is being presented as an entertainment more than mere information. It is as if television news has to be presented with this razzmatazz in order to be 'real'.

> *'If you didn't see it on the T.V. news, it didn't happen!'*

inquiry / enquiry (see enquiry, p. 49)

interior monologue (see also **point of view**, p. 104)

Interior monologue is one of the techniques by which *stream of consciousness* (see p. 106) is presented in fiction writing. It is used when someone speaks to himself or herself expressing his/her thoughts, and is written in the first person. It is the equivalent of *soliloquies* in the theatre where the character is alone on stage speaking his or her thoughts aloud.

interjection (from the Latin *inter*, meaning 'between' and *ject*, meaning 'throw')

Interjection is one of the eight parts of speech in traditional grammar, and means words that are 'thrown' into a sentence to express an emotion or claim someone's attention. Interjections are often single words and they need not be followed by an exclamation mark, but often are.

Hullo   Alas   Hooray!   Oh!   Coo-ee!   G'day

interrogative pronouns

Interrogative pronouns are called this because they *interrogate* or *question*. They are: *who, whom, whose, which, what, whoever, whichever, whatever*.

> *Which* is the house and *who* is going to be there?
> Out of the cars, *whose* are we going in and *what* does it look like?

intertextuality (from the Latin *inter*, meaning 'between' and *texere*, meaning 'compose')

Intertextuality is the term used to explain that any one text is always read, or created, in relation to other texts. This means that all readers bring to bear on texts a range of individual knowledge and understandings. Various associations and recognitions are made and the new text is understood in the light of previous textual experiences.

Viewing a film after reading the novel, or vice versa, is an example of applying intertextual knowledge. A comparison or contrast of how each is treated is made according to each individual's personal experiences and understandings.

intransitive verbs

Intransitive verbs are those which do not require a direct object to complete their meaning.

> He *sneezed* loudly.
> I *coughed* all through the performance.
> After a desperate struggle, she *fell* from the ledge.
> The sea *rose* like a mountain of water.

inverted commas (see quotation marks, p. 116)

invitation (written)

An **invitation** is a method of inviting someone to a special function or event. Invitations can take various forms and can be formal or informal. However, all invitations must contain specific details, such as
- the hosts (the *who*)
- occasion (the *what* and the *why*)
- the date and time (the *when*)
- venue (the *where*)
- dress requirements (the *how*)
- cost (if any)
- reply details (*RSVP*, see p. 124).

irony

Irony is the term used to describe a situation where the meaning of a statement is different from what is actually said or performed. It is derived from the Greek *eiron* which was a term used to refer to a dramatic character who pretended to be less intelligent than he really was.

There are various types of irony:
- *dramatic irony*
- *irony of situation*
- *tragic irony*
- *verbal irony*

(See also separate listings for these.)

irony of situation

Irony of situation occurs in its simplest form when one person's misfortune becomes a humorous situation for another who, unbeknown, is facing a similar misfortune. Many farces and comedies incorporate this irony of situation. It is very much 'he who laughs last, laughs loudest'.

Irony of situation is often more subtle than this, particularly when it occurs in novels such as *To Kill a Mockingbird* by Harper Lee. Several incidents in this novel are presented in an ironic light as a comment on the people of Maycomb.

One such example is the ironic situation of 'the most devout lady in Maycomb', Mrs Merriweather, at the Missionary Tea Party (p. 234), when she pontificates on the good fortunes of the blacks who are told to smile because 'Jesus Christ never went around grumbling and complaining'. This comment is made immediately after Tom Robinson, a negro, has been wrongfully convicted of raping a white woman, Mayella Ewell. The negro population is outraged.

italics

In printed works italics are used principally for
- titles of books, plays, films, poems and operas
- names of newspapers, magazines and periodicals
- names of ships
- foreign words and phrases
- emphasis.

Underlining is used in place of italics in handwritten work. It is incorrect to underline *and* use quotation marks for the one title.

it's / its

It's is the contraction for *it is*. The apostrophe notes the omission of the letter *i* in *is*.

> *It's* (it is) time that the dog came in; *it's* (it is) getting late.

Its is the possessive form of the pronoun *it* and has no apostrophe. It is the same for all possessive pronoun forms such as *hers, his, theirs, ours,* and *yours* — none has an apostrophe.

> *It's* (it is) time that the dog came in for *its* dinner.
> They think *it's* (it is) *theirs,* but I know *its* owner.

Remember:
- If the spoken *its* can be replaced with the words *it is,* then write *it's.*
- If not, then write *its.*

J

jargon

Jargon refers to the special language of a particular group or profession.

> We hear an economist talking of elastic demand, micro-economic reform, the heritage of institutional support, and a return to 'Fortress Australia'.

jingoism / jingoist (see also **chauvinism**, p. 25)

These words have been derived from the expression 'by jingo!' which occurred in a song sung by those who favoured sending the British fleet to attack the Russians in 1878. These people were militant zealots, blatantly bigoted in their patriotism, whose behaviour coined the words **jingoism/jingoist.** The words are still current today and refer to those who are extremely intolerant in their wish to support their country.

job applications

Job applications are probably some of the most important letters written.

Any job application should contain two parts:

1 a covering letter of application
2 a résumé or curriculum vitae.

A *covering letter* should
- be set out like a business letter (see **business letters**, p. 21)
- include the name and title of addressee
- open with *Dear Sir/Dear Madam* or addressee's name
- include in the first paragraph the position applied for, any reference number it may have, and when and where advertised
- state in the second paragraph the applicant's suitability and interest in the position
- refer in the third paragraph to the résumé/curriculum vitae enclosed and applicant's availability for an interview
- conclude *Yours faithfully* if addressed to *Dear Sir/Dear Madam*, or *Yours sincerely* if addressed to a particular person by name.

A *résumé/curriculum vitae* should include
- name, address and phone number
- date of birth
- details of education and any academic awards
- employment history, with dates and employers' names
- details of interests and any achievements in these areas
- names, addresses and positions of required referees
- date available to take up position.

Job applications should be neat, legible, correctly spelt and punctuated, and preferably typed.

journal

A **journal** is a form of writing that is more reflective than recording. The journal writers review personal experiences, feelings or events from the past and are commenting on these in relation to the present and future. Sometimes jokes, anecdotes conversations, poems and magazine cuttings are included. A good example of a novel written as a journal is *So much to tell you . . .* by John Marsden.

journalistic style

This term is used mainly for the *inverted pyramid* structure of most news reports. It is as if the news items are tapered, from the most important details down to the least important. The main components of the opening paragraphs are *who?*, *what?*, *where?*, *when?*, *why?*, *how?*

The reader learns
- *who* was involved
- *what* happened
- *where* it happened
- *when* it happened
- *why* it happened
- *how* it happened.

All this information is often presented in single-sentence paragraphs.

Different sections of the newspaper have different styles:
- factual/objective style for general news items, police and court reports, government and council announcements
- opinionative/interpretive style for editorials and feature articles
- expressive/emotive style for human interest stories
- sensational style for family tragedy, crimes and dramatic accidents
- appropriate jargon for particular sports with dramatic, interesting and exciting words that are familiar to the reader, literary terms to heighten effect and frequent use of clichés.

juxtaposition

Juxtaposition is the technique of placing close together, or side by side, events, characters or objects to emphasise or highlight some particular aspect. It can be used verbally or visually.

K

key words (see **note-making**, p. 87)

kind / kinds

Kind is a singular noun and should have the singular adjectives *this* or *that* before it.

> I don't like *this/that kind* of a meal.

Kinds is a plural noun and should have the plural adjectives *these* or *those* before it.

> *These/those kinds* of shoes are becoming very popular.

Never mix them, as in:

> *Those kind* of things annoy me.

This should be:

> *Those kinds* of things annoy me.

kind of / sort of

These are unnecessary expressions when used in such sentences as

> I *kind of* see what you mean.
> I *sort of* missed it.

which could be expressed as

> I see/understand what you mean.
> I just missed it.

L

lay / lie

Lay is a transitive verb and means to place, position, or organise. The words *laying* and *laid* are formed from it. As a transitive verb, it takes an object in sentences such as:

> The chicken *laid* an egg.
> Do you know how to *lay* bricks?
> He was *laying* the table for dinner.
> She has gone to the TAB to *lay* a bet.
> They *have laid* down standards of behaviour.

Lie is an intransitive verb and has two main meanings:

1 to speak untruthfully, which gives the forms *lying* and *lied*.

> He *lied* to his friends about the price of his bike.
> They knew we were *lying* about the incident.

2 to be at rest, repose, to be in a horizontal position, which gives the forms *lying*, *lay* and *lain*.

> The dog was *lying* on the mat.
> I *lie* in bed until the alarm goes off.
> The car has *lain* idle for many months.
> Exhausted, he *lay* down on the ground to rest.

● **Lie** can also be used as a noun in such sentences as:

> The *lie* of the ball caused problems for the golfer.
> Many of the rally drivers were defeated by the *lie* of the land.

lead / led

Lead can have three different meanings:

1 As a verb it means to show the way, guide, direct, and is pronounced *leed*. Its parts are *leads*, *leading* and *led*. **Led** has no other meaning but the past form of *lead* and is pronounced as it is spelt.

> He *led* his group in the wrong direction and became lost.
> The two cars *were leading* the pack until the last lap.
> We hope that the scout *leads* us to the lost explorer.

2 As a noun it can mean the principal role in a film or play; the main news story; an advantage over others; a wire cable; or a dog's leash.

All of these are pronounced *leed*.

> The *lead* in today's news was the death of the famous actor Sir Laurence
> Olivier, who took the *lead* in many plays and films.

3 As a noun and an adjective, it is used to describe the heavy metal
element *lead*, which is pronounced *led*.

> The quantity of *lead* in some paints has proved dangerous.
> She received a new box of *lead* pencils for a present.

legend

A **legend** is a story, originally in the oral tradition, that has been passed
down through the ages about the exploits of folk-heroes or events
which have been popularly accepted as history. We have legends based
on the exploits of Robin Hood, Ned Kelly, Helen Keller and Don
Bradman. The latter has become a legend in his own time.

lend / loan (see **borrow**, p. 20)

less / fewer (see **fewer**, p. 55)

letters

A **letter** is a written communication and, like all communications, it
requires you to consider three things: purpose, audience and form.

1 Why are you writing your letter? PURPOSE
2 Who will receive your letter? AUDIENCE
3 How will you present your letter? FORM

Purpose for the letter could be to complain, explain, inform,
congratulate, relate, entertain.

Audience for the letter could be friends, family, a business organisation, newspaper readers.

Form for the letter — depending on its *purpose* — will require a specific lay-out to make it acceptable.

There are various types of letters, such as:
- application (see **job applications**, p. 72)
- business (see **business letters**, p. 21 and **personal business letters**, p. 98)
- to the editor
- personal.

licence / license

Licence is the noun.

> You need a *licence* to drive a car.

License is the verb.

> Premises which sell alcohol have to be *licensed*.

License is used for both noun and verb in American English.

lie / lay (see **lay**, p. 76)

like

This word is not a conjunction, but it is frequently and incorrectly used as such in everyday conversation:

> It looks *like* it's going to rain.
> He ran *like* he's never run before.
> Why don't you do *like* I do?

In formal situations *as* or *as if / though* would be more correct.

> He stopped *as if* he were in pain.
> The car sounds *as though* it needs repairing.
> She found them to be a friendly group, *as* most Australians are.

Like can also be used as
- a preposition

> She speaks Italian *like* a native.
> He can swim *like* a fish.

- a noun

> I've never met his *like* before.
> His *likes* and dislikes are many.

- an adjective

> I've never seen anything *like* that.
> It's just *like* them to forget.

limerick

A **limerick** is a form of nonsense verse which follows the pattern:
- five lines
- lines 1, 2 and 5 rhyme; and lines 3 and 4 rhyme, i.e. a rhyme scheme
  a a b b a
- the poem's metre is three feet (trimeter) for lines 1, 2 and 5; and two
  feet (dimeter) for lines 3 and 4.

> There was a young man of Bengal
> Who went to a fancy dress ball
> He went, just for fun,
> Dressed up as a bun
> And a dog ate him up in the hall.
>
> Anonymous

limited point of view (see **point of view**, p. 104)

loan / lend (see **borrow**, p. 20)

loath / loth / loathe

Loath and **loth** are adjectives which mean unwilling, reluctant or
disinclined. Each of these is pronounced to rhyme with *oath*.

> She was *loath/loth* to continue her studies after failing her exams.
> I was *loath/loth* to give up my job and move away.

Loathe is a verb which means to detest, dislike strongly or to hate. It is
pronounced to rhyme with *clothe*.

> He began to *loathe* visiting his friend whose parents just ignored him.

He began to loathe visiting his friend,
whose parents just ignored him.

loose / lose (**loose** rhymes with *goose;* **lose** rhymes with *news*)

Loose as an adjective means free, not fitting closely, and not tight.

> There was a *loose* floorboard that squeaked when walked on.
> His *loose* belt told him that he was getting thinner.

Lose is a verb meaning not to win, or fail to keep, or to be without. Its forms are *loses, losing* and *lost.*

> The team will *lose* without its star player.
> My watch is *losing* a minute every hour.
> They *lost* their money at the races.

loose sentence

A **loose sentence** has the main clause coming first, followed by its subordinate clause(s). The sentence could end at one or more places before the full stop. For example:

> The ABC will move this new programme to another time-slot (**could end here**) because it can be combined without loss to an already existing programme (**could end here**) which is very popular.

The opposite to a loose sentence is a *periodic sentence* (see **periodic sentence**, p. 97).

lyric

The **lyric** was defined by the early Greeks as the expression of emotion of a single singer accompanied by a lyre. In modern terms it is still the expression of the poet's emotions about a topic or subject but, while it is no longer designed to be sung to an accompaniment, the lyric poem is essentially melodic and achieved by a variety of rhythm patterns.

M

main clause (see also **clause**, p. 26)

A **main clause** is a clause that can become a simple sentence in its own right.

> *He left early* (**main clause, stands on its own**) *because the others had gone.* (**subordinate clause, cannot stand on its own**)

main idea / topic sentence (see also **paragraph**, p. 94)

The **main idea** or **topic sentence** carries the most important piece of information for the reader. All the other sentences in the paragraph elaborate on this main idea and are known as the *supporting detail*. The main idea/topic sentence usually comes in the opening sentence of the paragraph, but it can occur during the paragraph or even at the end.

> *Life can be very tough in the first week of a lamb's life.* (**main idea/topic sentence**) There's the cold weather to endure, because it's June and July. Floods may come and wash them away. Crows and foxes are always looking for food; and brothers and sisters compete to survive. The weak ones will lose the fight. (**supporting detail**)

Life can be very tough in the first week of a lamb's life.

making notes (see **note-making**, p. 87)

malapropism (from the French *mal a propos*, meaning 'not to the purpose')

Malapropism is the inappropriate use of words which are confused because of the similarity of how they look or sound. The term is named after Mrs Malaprop, a character in Sheridan's play, 'The Rivals', who was forever confusing words.

> I am not under the *affluence* (influence) of alcohol.

may / can (see **can**, p. 23)

me / I (see **I**, p. 65)

media

This is the plural form of the word *medium,* which in Latin means
'middle'. The term is used mainly to refer to newspapers, magazines,
television, radio, film and video as the ways in which something is
communicated. In other words, the *medium* is what comes in the middle
between the person sending the message (the *transmitter*) and the
person receiving the message (the *receiver*).

    medium (singular): *one* way of sending a communication
    media (plural): *more* than one way of sending a communication

The term *mass media* means that a number of different media are being
used in order to reach a large number, or mass, of the population. It is a
'mass of media for the masses'!

melodrama (from the Greek word *melos,* meaning 'song')

The term **melodrama** originally applied to all musical plays, including
opera. Now, however, it is used to describe drama that is full of
sensational incident, flat characters, little convincing motivation and
with constant appeal to the emotions of the audience. The plot revolves
around malevolent intrigue and violent action. The characters (who are
very good, or *very* bad) are seen to be rewarded or punished. Poetic
justice is superficially achieved.

metaphor (see also **mixed metaphor**, p. 83)

Metaphor is a figure of speech in the form of a comparison. It is when
one thing is said to be something else.

    He was a tornado blasting his way through the opposing team.

metre (from the Greek *metron,* meaning 'measure')

Metre refers to the pattern of stressed and unstressed syllables in
poetry. A line of poetry may have a fixed number of syllables but have
a varying number of stresses. A poem usually keeps to one specific
metre form.

A *metric line* is named according to the number of feet in a line:

- monometer　　　1
- dimeter　　　　2
- trimeter　　　　3

- tetrameter   4
- pentameter   5
- hexameter   6
- heptameter   7
- octometer   8

minutes

The **minutes** are the written record which is kept of all official meetings of an organised group. They include details of date, time, venue, who attended, motions moved, passed and carried, rescinded, defeated, items discussed and correspondence received.

mixed metaphor

Mixed metaphor refers to several metaphors mixed without a common comparison. Mixed metaphors are often clumsy in their imagery and are seldom effective in their intentions.

> The mining company *was keeping a low profile* in order to get the new mine *off the ground*.
> They were doing their best *to iron out* all *the bottlenecks* in the system.
> He *spilt the beans* and *opened up a can of worms*.

mock heroic

This term is used interchangeably with *mock epic* and applies to the form of poetry which uses high-sounding language to trivialise or burlesque a topic or subject. The characteristics of the classical epic are used, such as the *epic formulas*, to make a subject ridiculous:
- the invocation to a deity
- formal statement of theme
- grandiose speeches of the heroes
- descriptions of warriors
- supernatural machinery

These are just some of the devices employed. Alexander Pope's 'The Rape of the Lock' is considered one of the finest examples of a mock heroic poem in English. It satirises, in polished verse, the trivialities of polite society in the eighteenth century and two families in dispute over the cutting of a lock of a lady's hair by a suitor.

mood (in literature)

This term refers to the emotional mood, or atmosphere, evoked by a written work. It is the use of word pictures to create an atmosphere of suspense, joy, tension, fear, sadness and so on.

Often the setting combines with the events to create a particular mood or atmosphere which can be referred to as a *sympathetic setting*. Such a combination operates in the opening scene of *Hamlet* where the guard is nervous and apprehensive before the ghost appears. In Thomas Hardy's *Tess of the d'Urbervilles* we read:

> Amid the oozing fatness and warm ferments of the Froom Vale, at a season when the rush of juices could almost be heard below the hiss of fertilization, it was impossible that the most fanciful love should not grow passionate. The ready bosoms existing there were impregnated by their surroundings. (ch. 24)

Hardy creates this setting to reinforce the thoughts and feelings of the characters and to foreshadow the emerging relationship between Tess and Angel.

mood (in verbs)

The **mood in verbs** indicates one of the four forms that a verb can take to express a particular state of mind or manner. These are:

1 *imperative,* which expresses a command.

Stop that!

2 *indicative,* which states a fact or poses a question.

Where is she?

3 *infinitive,* which is the base form.

To err is human.

4 *subjunctive,* which shows a wish, condition, or purpose.

I suggest that he be allowed to go.

motif

Motif is a repeated element of a pattern which can also be described as a minor theme. It is used to give unity to the writing or to help organise its ideas. In literature, motifs recur to link parts of the writing and give more force or focus to the central idea. One example of a motif is the repeated use of images such as 'night', 'blood' and 'hell', balanced against 'peace', 'sleep' and 'gentleness' in Shakespeare's *Macbeth*. These act as useful signposts to the central meaning of the play.

A more recent example is *The Green Piper* by Victor Kelleher, where the motif is Robert Browning's 'Pied Piper of Hamelin', which provides the main unifying thread to the story and links its parts.

myth (from the Greek word *mythos,* meaning 'a story')

This is one of the earliest forms of story-telling, and has developed because people have felt the need to tell about their world. Myths often form the basis of a society's culture and influence the way people behave in that society.

There are two main kinds of myth:

- **explanatory myths** when people long ago sought simple answers to questions about the world and themselves. To answer these questions they usually gave an explanation based on imagination. This formula succinctly illustrates this idea:

    QUESTION + IMAGINATION = MYTH

  The aboriginal myth 'How the Sun Was Made' is an example of an explanatory myth.

- **aesthetic myths** are merely to entertain and delight the listener. These often told stories about gods and what had to be done to please them. Many aesthetic myths are just beautiful stories which have been passed down to us over thousands of years. The Greek myth 'Orpheus and Eurydice' is one such myth.

N

narrative

Narrative is any form of prose or verse writing that tells a story. It is not limited by length. *Narrative poetry* is a generic term for all types of poems that tell a story. (Epics and ballads are two of the more common forms of narrative poems.)

narrator

Narrator is the term applied to the story-teller who recounts a narrative, either in writing or orally. As well as having narrators in prose and verse, a narrator is sometimes used in drama to introduce or explain scenes and/or events.

In fiction the 'I' who tells the story is the narrator, who does not always have to be the central character (the protagonist), but may be an observer, or a minor character. The author's use of 'I' should not necessarily be regarded as representing the author (see **persona**, p. 97). While a narrator is always present, at least by implication, in a work of fiction he or she is not always apparent. **Point of view**, (p. 104) explains the non-obvious narrator more fully.

neither / either (see **either/neither**, p. 47)

neither / nor (see **either/or**, p. 47)

none

The word **none** may mean *not one* or *not any*.

- If *not one* is intended, then the subject and verb are in the *singular*.
    None of the bottles *has* been opened.
- If *not any* is intended, then the subject and verb are in the *plural*.
    None of my friends *have* visited me.

non-fiction

Non-fiction refers to a factual piece of writing which may be scientific, scholarly or didactic and covers forms such as treatises, histories, biographies, encyclopaedic entries and so on.

non-print media (see also **media**, p. 82)

Non-print media refers to electronic media such as television, radio, film and video.

note-making / note-taking

This is an important skill used in researching, reporting and summarising. Note-making relies upon the selection of main ideas and supporting details in paragraphs. Once these have been written down they form the basis for a set of notes. There are three main methods for note-making:

Method One

- Skim read to determine what the passage is all about.
- Correctly record factual information, such as dates, numbers, names and places.
- If using the author's words, put them in quotation marks.
- Select main ideas and supporting details by emphasising key words and phrases.
- Express ideas as briefly and concisely as possible.

Method Two

- Organise notes on a passage by underlining key words and phrases.

Method Three

- As mentioned in Method One, any words or phrases copied verbatim from texts must be acknowledged as someone else's by enclosing them in quotation marks. One way of gathering information from reference books and not plagiarising an author's work is to work with two columns:

Notes from the book	Own interpretation

noun

The **noun** is one of the parts of speech and names a
- person (proper nouns)
    Bill   Fiona   David
- place (proper nouns)
    Adelaide   Perth   Melbourne
- thing (common nouns)
    pencil   book   chair
- quality (abstract nouns)
    beauty   greed   love
- collection (collective nouns)
    team   class   club

(See separate listings for each kind of noun.)

noun clause

The **noun clause** acts like a noun and is usually introduced by
that   what   who   which   where   when   how   why

It may be
- a subject of a verb
    What is happening (**noun clause**) worries me.
    noun clause = subject of verb *worries*.
- an object of a verb
    I note *that he is late again* (**noun clause**).
    noun clause = object of verb *note*.
- an object of a preposition
    We can tell by *what he is doing* (**noun clause**).
    noun clause = object of preposition *by*.
- a complement of the verb 'to be'
    It is *where I expected to find it* (**noun clause**).
    noun clause = complement of verb *is*.

noun phrase

The **noun phrase** usually includes some form of the verb. It may be

- an infinitive subject

  To offer so much (**noun phrase**) is very generous.

- a gerund subject

  Exercising too long (**noun phrase**) may be dangerous.

- an infinitive object

  She tried *to join the hockey team* (**noun phrase**).

- a preposition object

  He has the excuse of *being unwell* (**noun phrase**).

noun verbal (see **gerund,** p. 60)

novel (from the Italian *novella,* meaning 'a new tale')

The term **novel** came into the English language in the sixteenth century. It was during that time that various stories such as *Decameron* and *Don Quixote* were being translated into English from their Italian and Spanish origins. The English novel had its beginnings around the eighteenth century. Examples of early English novels are:

Pilgrim's Progress by John Bunyan (1678)
Robinson Crusoe by Daniel Defoe (1719)
Moll Flanders by Daniel Defoe (1722)
Gulliver's Travels by Jonathan Swift (1726)
Pamela; or Virtue Rewarded by Samuel Richardson (1741)

The term is used to describe any extended fictional prose narrative that is a representation of life or experience. It is customary for the novel's narrative to encompass character(s) who experience, or engage in, events which may cause them to change or develop. There is usually some organising principle such as a *plot* and/or *theme.*

NOVEL STUDY PRO FORMA

Ask these questions when reading a novel:

Setting (see p. 127)
- What is the time and place of the story?
- Do these have any bearing on or importance to the story?
- Does the setting vary, or is it static?
- Are characters affected by the setting? How?

Mood/Atmosphere (see p. 84)
- Is there a particular atmosphere created?
- How is this created?
- What effect does it have on characters and events?

Characters (see p. 24)
- What does the author tell us about the character(s), i.e. 'descriptive' presentation?
- What do the characters reveal about themselves by what they think, say and do, i.e. the 'dramatic' presentation?
- How do the characters respond to stress and conflict?
- What do others think of particular characters and their relationships?
- How do the characters change or develop?

Conflict (see p. 33)
- Is the character in conflict with (an)other character(s)?
- What form does this conflict take?
- Does the character face an inner conflict?
- Is there some conflict with an outside force or nature?
- Is the character in conflict with the values or attitudes of society?
- Is the conflict resolved? How?
- What effect does the conflict have on the character and/or events?

Point of View (see p. 104)
- Is the story told in the first person point of view (I/we), or third person point of view (he/she/they)?
- Does this affect the reader's understanding of the story?

Style (see p. 140)
- What is the form of narration — diary, flashback, narrative prose?
- How is language being used — sentence structure, vocabulary?
- What devices or techniques are employed — imagery, contrasts, repetition, symbol?

Theme (see p. 149)
- Is a comment being made on some particular aspect of life?
- Is some message being implied by the sequence of events?

novella (from the Italian meaning 'a little new thing')

The term **novella** originally referred to the early tales of Italian and French writers. We now use it to refer to a short novel.

numbers

Numbers may be expressed in figures as well as written in full according to the context, writer's style or publisher's requirements. Usual practices are:

• figures for mathematical, scientific, technical and commercial texts
• figures for sums of money, page numbers, dates and time
• a combination of figures and words for very large numbers, such as *$18.5 million*
• when two numbers come together, put one in figures and the other in words, such as *two 40-horsepower motors*
• avoid using a figure for opening a sentence and write the word instead, such as *Six people are here today.*
• be consistent in keeping to figures or words, such as *two to five age range*, or *2 to 5 age range*.

number of

• The phrase **a number of** usually indicates a *plural subject* and so must take a *plural verb*.

  A number of people *have* been killed.

  He saw that *a number of* students *were* not attending.

• The phrase **the number of** usually indicates a *singular subject* and so must take a *singular verb*.

  The number of accidents *is* alarming.

  She will check and find *the number of* absences *has* increased.

O

object (in sentences)

The **object in sentences** usually comes after the verb and is the person
or thing affected by the action. To determine the object it helps to ask
what or *who* has been affected by the verb.

The dog *chased* (**what?**) *his tail* (**object**).
The dog *chased* (**whom?**) *the man* (**object**).
I saw (**what?**) *the fight* (**object**).
He rang (**what?**) *the bell* (**object**).
She asked (**whom?**) *Marie* (**object**).

objective writing

Objective writing is free of personal feelings and emotions, so that the
views offered are without opinion or personal prejudice. News
reporting, as well as all other forms of factual, informative writing
should be objective.

ode

Ode denotes an elaborate lyric poem which addresses someone or
something in sincere and dignified language. Originally it was a Greek
form used in dramatic poetry and choral in quality. Some well-known
odes are:

'To a Skylark', Percy Bysshe Shelley
'Ode on a Grecian Urn', John Keats
'Ode: Imitations of Immortality', William Wordsworth

of / off / have

- **Of** is a preposition which is pronounced *ov*, as in

a glass *of* water
a pile *of* wood

- **Off** may be a preposition, an adverb or an adjective. It is pronounced
to rhyme with *scoff.*

He jumped *off* (**preposition**) the wall.
She got ten per cent *off* (**adverb**).
The milk is *off* (**adjective**).

- **Off** should not be followed by *from* or *of.*

He jumped *off* (of) the wall.   (Omit *of*)
He jumped *off* (from) the wall.   (Omit *from*)

- **Have** is a verb and frequently in conversation it is contracted to *'ve* and is pronounced similarly to *of*. But in written form *of* cannot replace *have* or *'ve*. It is incorrect to use a preposition as a substitute for a verb.

He should *(ha)'ve* helped me.	(Not *of!*)
They could *(ha)'ve* told us.	(Not *of!*)
You might *(ha) 've* told me.	(Not *of!*)

omniscient (see **point of view**, p. 104)

onomatopoeia

Onomatopoeia refers to words whose meaning is suggested in their pronunciation (sound). Some onomatopoeic words are:

hiss slam buzz whirr sizzle boom

It is a poetic technique used by writers to add extra effect and dimension to their work.

> The buzz saw snarled and rattled in the yard
> And made dust and dropped stove-length sticks of wood
> Robert Frost, 'Out, Out —'

opinion / fact (see **fact/opinion**, p. 54)

opinionative writing

Opinionative writing is expository writing of a personal kind. It is shaped by the writer's particular viewpoint or opinion on the topic. The writer expresses a judgement, makes recommendations and takes a particular stance on the topic. It is very much a subjective approach and assessment of the subject.

oral / aural (see **aural/oral**, p. 16)

oxymoron

This term refers to two contradictory words which are used to create a sharp emphasis through contrast or *antithesis*.

cheerful pessimist
wise fool
sad joy
eloquent silence

P

parable

A **parable** is a short story which illustrates a moral or lesson. The most well-known parables are those told by Christ, such as the story of the sower, and of the good Samaritan.

paradox

Paradox is a rhetorical device used to attract a reader's attention, and a statement which, while seemingly contradictory or absurd, contains an element of truth.

> *None so credulous as infidels.*
> *It's a wise man who knows his own son.*

paragraph (from the Greek words *para*, meaning 'beside/near/alongside' and *graph*, meaning 'write')

The word **paragraph** was originally used by the Greeks to indicate a break in a play script. By presenting written work in paragraphs today, the writer is giving the reader a short break between ideas. Important points to note are:

- each paragraph starts on a new line and may be indented
- there is a main idea or topic sentence in each paragraph
- the topic sentence is often the opening sentence
- the other sentences offer supporting detail
- generally, paragraphs have from two to ten sentences
- a one-sentence paragraph is a journalistic style.

parallel sentence

This is a 'balanced' sentence in that it has the same structure before and after a conjunction such as *and, but, or*.

> He likes *swimming* (**participle**) *and playing* (**participle**) football.

The sentence would not be balanced if it were written:

> He likes *swimming* (**participle**) and *to play* (**infinitive**) football.

Sentences should be balanced and have parallel structures whenever these are needed.

> He is *tall, slim* (**adjectives**) and *a person of great attraction* (**phrase**).

should be rewritten as:

> He is *tall, slim* (**adjectives**), and *very attractive* (**adjective**).

paraphrase (from the Latin *paraphrasis*, meaning 'recount')

Paraphrasing is used today to describe a recounting or expressing of some topic in words other than the original but with the same meaning. The intention is to clarify the topic's meaning and to indicate that it has been understood.

parenthesis (see **brackets**, p. 21)

parody

A **parody** is a humorous imitation of a particular writer's style, somewhat like a *caricature*. It entertains by emphasising certain features of the original in a humorous way. The original is often serious in what it expresses; the parody sets out to achieve the opposite.

participles

Participles are formed from verbs. There are two kinds:

1 **present participle**, which is the verb form that ends in *-ing*
   walking   driving   being   looking   wondering

2 **past participle**, which is the verb form that usually ends in *-ed*, or *-t*, but may be formed in other ways
   looked   burnt   learnt   loved   caught   gone   been

parts of speech

There are eight **parts of speech**:
- *adjective*
- *adverb*
- *conjunction*
- *interjection*

● *noun*

● *preposition*

● *pronoun*

● *verb*

(See separate listings for each of these.)

These labelling names are given to the words in a sentence in an attempt to understand how language functions. The intention is to clarify the *part* that each word plays as it contributes towards the *total* meaning of the sentence. The same word may be used in different sentences in different ways.

> Look at his *back* **(noun).**
> She *backed* **(verb)** the car.
> Here are *back* **(adjective)** copies of the magazine.
> Put the book *back* **(adverb).**

passed / past

Passed is the past participle formed from the verb *pass*.

> Time *passed* slowly.
> She has *passed* her examinations.

It can be used only as a verb.

Past may be

● an adjective

> for the *past* year

● a noun

> in the *past*

● an adverb

> The bird flew *past*.

passive voice

The **passive voice** of the verb is being used when the *subject* of the sentence receives the *action* of the verb.

> The jug *has been broken* by the cat.
> The holiday *was spoilt* by the rain.
> They *will be disappointed* by the news.

Points to note :

● **Passive voice** is usually formed from part of the verb *to be* plus the past participle.

● The subject of the passive verb is the direct object when the sentence is put into the active voice.

> The cat *has broken* the jug **(active).**
> The jug *has been broken* by the cat **(passive).**

pastoral

Pastoral is a form of literature (commonly poetic), which presents aspects of the life of rustics: shepherds and creatures of the fields. The form began in the third century BC when the Sicilian poet Theocritus included poetic sketches of rural life in his *Idylls*.

past tense

The **past tense** is the form of the verb used to express an action that happened in the past. There are four main past tenses:

1 simple past

> He *watched* the game.

2 continuous past

> He *was watching* the game.

3 perfect past

> He *has watched* the game.

4 pluperfect past

> He *had watched* the game.

pentameter (from the Greek words *penta*, meaning 'five' and *meter*, meaning 'measure')

The term **pentameter** is used to describe a line of verse that contains five metrical feet. These are usually *iambic*.

> When I / do count / the clock / that tells / the time. /
>   Shakespeare

periodic sentence

A **periodic sentence** has the subordinate clause(s) coming first and the main clause coming at the end. The meaning is not completed until the end of the sentence.

> Since there is a very popular programme which could be combined with the new programme, the ABC intends to move this to the other time-slot.

Too many periodic sentences make for heavy going. They are the opposite of *loose sentences* (see p. 80)

persona

The term **persona** is used to designate the author in his or her role of storyteller/narrator. In some cases the persona is an unseen voice; in others it appears as a nameless 'I'. (When the narrator of a story is an actual character, the term does not apply.) The term **persona** should not be confused with the author in real life; instead it should be regarded as a mask the author puts on.

personal / personnel

Personal is an adjective meaning matters that are private to a particular individual.

> This is for your *personal* use.
> It's a *personal* matter.

The stress is on the first syllable — *per*-sonal.

Personnel can be used as an adjective and a noun, meaning the people employed in a particular organisation, such as the staff.

> More *personnel* are needed to cope with the heavy workload.
> They applied to the *Personnel* Manager for the vacancies.

The stress is on the final syllable — person-*nel*.

personal business letters

These are written by private individuals for conducting personal business matters. They may be sent to banks, businesses, government departments and other official organisations. You should quote any reference details such as account number etc. Personal business letters may be either typed or handwritten. Usually the letter will begin: *Dear Sir/Madam* and conclude *Yours faithfully*. Remember to keep a copy of your letter.

In the absence of a letterhead it is necessary to include one's name and address. The following are examples of acceptable forms of layout:

1 Placed at the top right-hand side of the page:

Name may be omitted if given under ⟶ Mr J J Citizen
signature at end of letter.   16 Smith Crescent
                                              HOMETOWN VIC 3990

1 October 1992

The Manager
Commonwealth Bank of Australia
Main Street
DOWNTOWN   VIC   3000

2 Placed at the top left-hand side of the page:

Mrs J. J. Citizen   ⟵ Name may be omitted if given
16 Smith Crescent   under signature at end of letter.
HOMETOWN VIC 3990

1 October 1992

Registrar of Motor Vehicles
60 Moorefield Road
MELBOURNE VIC 3000

3 Blocked at left-hand margin beneath writer's signature:

Yours faithfully

Jane Citizen

Ms Jane Citizen
16 Smith Crescent
HOMETOWN VIC 3990

personal letters

These are written in a friendly and natural style. They express the writer's thoughts and feelings and are of interest to the receiver because they deal with shared topics. They are conversational or chatty in their tone and often reveal the writer's character. The salutation is usually *Dear Jane* or *Dear Craig* and the complimentary close can be in a variety of forms, such as:

Yours sincerely	Yours	Lots of love
Your friend	Regards	Yours lovingly

personal pronoun

The **personal pronoun** is used in place of a noun that refers to the name of a person, place or thing. A personal pronoun can be either the *subject*, the *object*, or the *possessive* form.

SUBJECT	OBJECT	POSSESSIVE
I	me	mine
you	you	yours
he	him	his
she	her	hers
it	it	its
we	us	ours
they	them	theirs

Remember: prepositions take the *object* form of the personal pronoun, so the following should be used:

It is between *you* and *me*.
This is for *you* and *him*.
He was with Julie and *us*.
Give it to Bill and *them*.

personification

Personification occurs when writers describe an animal or an object as if it were a person. They give it human qualities and bring it to life, for example by saying that it *walks, smiles, frowns, rages, mutters, dances*.

persuade / convince (see **convince**, p. 35)

persuasive writing

Persuasive writing works upon the receiver's senses in order to influence his or her feelings. It is usually emotive in its context, such as in advertisements, and appeals to instincts such as fear, greed, status or sex. Good persuasive writing is often a mix of reason and emotion, appealing to the head as well as the heart. Anecdotes, humour and personal experiences are often included to persuade the receiver that the writer's thoughts and feelings are justified. *Speeches, argumentative* and *opinionative* writing fit into this category.

Petrarchan sonnet (see also **sonnet**, p. 130)

The **Petrarchan sonnet** originated in Italy during the Renaissance (14th century) from the Italian poet Petrarch, and was later developed and varied by the English sonneteers.

phrase

A **phrase** is a group of related words that make a meaningful contribution to a sentence. A phrase cannot stand on its own and must not be used as a sentence.

> The boy climbed *to the top of the hill.*

The phrase *to the top of the hill* has no verb and is not a sentence.

The position of a phrase in a sentence is important.

> My mother bought a coat for my sister *with a fur lining.*

The phrase *with a fur lining* needs to come immediately after 'coat'.

(See also separate listings under **adjectival phrase, adverbial phrase, noun phrase, prepositional phrase, verb phrase.**)

plagiarism

Plagiarism occurs when another's literary work is copied by someone and passed off as his or her own, without acknowledging its original source. This is regarded as a serious offence.

plot

The **plot** is the sequence of events in any narrative that unfolds as we read. It may be organised in various ways by the writer to maintain readers' interest in the story. (See also **sub-plot**, p. 143)

plurals (of nouns)

Plurals are formed by
- adding *-s* to the singular
    cups books horses
- adding *-es* to words ending in s, sh, ch, z, or x
    matches buses boxes *waltzes* lashes
- changing *y* to *ies* when a consonant comes before *y*
    ladies spies worries

- changing *f* to *ves* for words such as
    wi*ves* kni*ves* sel*ves* cal*ves* hal*ves* loa*ves*
- adding *-es* to words ending in *o*, such as
    carg*oes* ding*oes* her*oes* negr*oes* potat*oes* tomat*oes* volcan*oes*

Dingoes

- recognising the Greek or Latin origins of words like:
phenomenon	phenomen*a*
criterion	criteri*a*
datum	dat*a*
maximum	maxim*a*
minimum	minim*a*
stratum	strat*a*
radius	radi*i*
locus	loc*i*
terminus	termin*i*
medium	medi*a*

- changing *is* to *es*
analysis	analys*es*
axis	ax*es*
basis	bas*es*
crisis	cris*es*
hypothesis	hypothes*es*
oasis	oas*es*
thesis	thes*es*

poetry

Poetry is a term applied to the many forms which are rhythmic expressions of imaginative and intense perceptions or experiences of the world. It is one of the most personal forms of expressions there is, with poets choosing their words carefully and economically. They create images and feelings with words, just as a painter creates a picture with colours.

The following are just some of the ways people have tried to define poetry:

Poetry is the imaginative expression of strong feeling, usually rhythmical. . .the spontaneous overflow of powerful feelings recollected in tranquillity.
William Wordsworth

I would define the poetry of words as the rhythmical creation of beauty. Its sole arbiter is taste. With the intellect or with the conscience it has only collateral relations. Unless incidentally, it has no concern whatever either with duty or with truth.
Edgar Allan Poe

Poetry is the record of the best and happiest moments of the best and happiest minds.
Shelley

I wish our clever young poets would remember my homely definitions of prose and poetry; that is prose: words in their best order; poetry: the best words in the best order.
Samuel Taylor Coleridge

By poetry we mean the art of employing words in such a manner as to produce an illusion of the imagination, the art of doing by means of words what the painter does by means of colours.
Macaulay

Poetry, therefore, we will call musical Thought.
Carlyle

The art which uses words as both speech and song to reveal the realities that the senses record, the feelings salute, the mind perceives, and the shaping imagination orders.
Babette Deutsch

Poetry is, first and last, lived experience, not something out of a refrigerator; the more clearly it is relived, on the page or on the stage, the more successful it is and always will be.
Bruce Dawe

POETRY STUDY PRO FORMA

Ask these questions when reading a poem:

Theme (see p. 149)
- What is the poem about?
- Is there one or more main idea/theme?
- What was the poet's purpose/intention?

Form
- What form of poem is it? Ballad, sonnet, interior monologue, free verse?
- Is the form used to support the theme or to contrast for added emphasis/impact?

Style (see p. 140)
- What contribution does rhythm make?
- Is there a definite rhyme scheme?
- How is the poem structured? What is the line and stanza length?
- What devices/techniques/figures of speech are used?
- How do these contribute to imagery, sound effects, musical qualities, and the reader's emotional responses?
- Are there specific symbols?

Mood/atmosphere (see p. 84)
- Is there a strong mood/atmosphere created?
- How is language used to create this?
- Is the reader influenced to make a particular response?

point of view

In everyday conversation, **point of view** means somebody's opinion or views on a topic. The expression 'from my point of view' indicates that we are about to give our opinion or say what we think. When we use point of view in discussing a piece of writing we are referring to whoever is telling the story. Every story must be told through somebody's eyes — those of the narrator, who relates what is seen and heard. It is the narrator's interpretation that becomes the point of view in a story.

Point of view, then, is an important part of story-telling, and it influences the understanding that the reader gets of events, character motivation, suspense, conflict and theme.

There are two main kinds of point of view — *first* and *third* — and within these two broad categories the following types of narration may be found:

First person
This refers to the use of *I* — the first-person pronoun — to tell the story.
- *subjective* The narrator is a major or minor character in the story who reports the events as if they had just happened and who appears to be unaware of the full meaning of the events. The reader knows more than the narrator.
- *detached* The narrator is a major character in the story who recalls the events from the vantage point of maturity. He has had time to reflect on the meaning of the events. This is reflective writing and is a retrospective view of what happened.
- *observer* The narrator is a minor character in the story who plays the roles of eyewitness and confidant. His or her sources of information are what he or she hears and sees and what the main character tells him or her.

In all of these, the reader's understanding of events is restricted, because the reader lives, acts, feels and shares only the narrator's experiences and confidences.

Third person
This refers to the use of *he, she, they* to tell the story.
- *omniscient* (from the Latin *omni*, meaning 'all', and *sciere*, meaning 'know', thus 'all-knowing') The narrator is capable of knowing, seeing, and telling whatever he or she wishes in the story, and exercises this freedom at will. It is characterised by freedom in shifting from the exterior world to the inner selves of a number of characters and by freedom in movement in time and place. The author chooses this method of narration in order to be free to comment upon the meaning of actions, and to state the thematic intentions of the story at will.
- *intrusive* As above, but also includes comments on the characters' actions and therefore makes judgements on and about them.
- *limited* The narrator sees and reports the action through the eyes of one character who is limited in what is experienced, thought and felt.

Stream of consciousness is a term coined by William James in *Principles of Psychology* (1890). It is a technique used by a writer for presenting the psychological aspects of a character's thoughts and actions, and the unbroken flow of ideas, information, hopes and fears that are going on in a person's mind. It can be presented in either *first* or *third person point of view*. The beginning of James Joyce's *A Portrait of the Artist as a Young Man* is an example of this technique.

● *Interior monologue* is one of the techniques of **stream of consciousness** and is presented in *first person* (see **interior monologue**, p. 69).

possessive apostrophe

The **possessive apostrophe** is used after a noun in order to show that something is owned or possessed by that noun. This could be indicated by the word *of,* but the possessive apostrophe is frequently used in spoken and written forms.

● Singular nouns have **apostrophe** + *s*:

the coat *of* Diane	*Diane's* coat
the lead *of* the dog	the *dog's* lead
a holiday *of* one week	one *week's* holiday
prices *of* last year	last *year's* prices

● Plural nouns may or may not have **apostrophe** + *s*:

the hats *of* the ladies	the *ladies'* hat
shouting *of* the boys	the *boys'* shouting
the bells *of* the churches	the *churches'* bells
noise *of* the children	the *children's* noise
coats *of* the women	the *women's* coats

Important points to note:

● The apostrophe is added to the base noun.
● The base noun may be singular or plural, but it will always be followed by an apostrophe.
● If an *s* is sounded after the base noun, then add *s*.
● If no *s* is sounded, do not put one.

Rules to follow:

● Determine the base noun, which may be singular or plural.
● Add an apostrophe to the base noun.
● If an *s* is sounded, add *s*.
● If no *s* is sounded, do not put one.

possessive pronouns

Possessive pronouns indicate ownership or possession. These are:

> *mine   yours   his   hers   its   ours   theirs*

- Possessive pronouns do not have an apostrophe.

    > That dog of *yours* is always wagging *its* tail wildly.
    > I think that's *hers; ours* is over there.

- Do not use an apostrophe with pronouns ending in *-self* or *-selves*.

    > We have nobody but *ourselves* to blame for the problem.
    > It is necessary to look after *oneself* to keep fit.

- There are no such words as *hisself* or *theirselves;* it should be *himself* or *themselves*.

practice / practise

Practice is the noun.

> It is said that *practice* makes perfect.

Practise is the verb.

> When he *practised* on his drum-kit, the neighbours complained.

Practice is used for both noun and verb in American English.

predicate (pronounced *prediket*)

In traditional grammar the **predicate** is that part of a clause or sentence which indicates what happened to the subject. The predicate is what is left after the subject has been removed.

> The golfer (**subject**) *hit the ball straight into the bunker* (**predicate**).
> The two ladies (**subject**) *were walking slowly down the road* (**predicate**).
> They (**subject**) *were watching* (**predicate**), but the thief (**subject**) *didn't know* (**predicate**).

Note: The predicate always includes the finite verb and offers information about the subject.

prefix

A **prefix** is a word or element that is placed at the *beginning* of a root word to form a new meaning. Most prefixes are from Latin or Greek. Common prefixes are:

anti	against/opposite, as in *antiseptic, antidote*
auto	self, as in *automatic, autograph*
inter	between, as in *interrupt, interfere*
semi	half, as in *semicircle, semicolon*
trans	across, as in *transport, transfer*

preposition

A **preposition** is used with a noun or pronoun to indicate the noun or pronoun's relationship to some other word in the sentence. This may be:

- a verb and a noun

     The boat sank (**verb**) *after* (**preposition**) the storm (**noun**).

- an adjective and a noun

     Sad (**adjective**) *at* (**preposition**) his loss (**noun**), he went home.

- another noun or pronoun

     She saw the book (**noun**) *on* (**preposition**) the table (**noun**).

In the last sentence, the preposition *on* can be seen as indicating the position of the book, with *pre* meaning 'before' and *position* meaning 'place'. A number of other prepositions could be substituted for *on*, such as *under, by, below, behind* and *beside*. This shows that a preposition is always expressing a positional and connecting relationship; otherwise, it is not a preposition.

     She jumped *over* (**preposition**) the fence.
     They fell *over* (**adverb**).
     The cricketer bowled an *over* (**noun**).

- *Remember*, ALL prepositions take an *object*.

     He spoke *to* (**preposition**) *you and me* (**object**).
     It is *for* (**preposition**) *them and us* (**object**) to decide.

- It has been said that a preposition should not be used to end a sentence. It is difficult to justify this. As Winston Churchill once said:

     This is the sort of English up with which I shall not put.

- Prepositions can be overused, as illustrated by what a boy said to his mother:

     "What did you want to bring the book I didn't want to be read *to out of up for* (**prepositions**)?"

prepositional phrase

A **prepositional phrase** starts with a preposition such as *in, on, to, from, with, by, between* and *near*. This is followed by a noun or pronoun which is the *object* of the preposition.

     in the future
     on this occasion
     with you and me
     near us

present participle

The **present participle** is formed by the addition of *-ing* to the verb.

run	*running*
walk	*walking*
receive	*receiving*

- If a sentence starts with a present participle, then the participle must relate to the subject in the main clause.

    Walking down the road, *he* met his sister (**main clause**).

In other words this means:

    As he was walking down the road he met his sister.

Now read this sentence:

    Walking down the road, *my nose* felt cold.

In other words this would mean:

    As my nose was walking down the road it felt cold.

This sentence needs rewording. One way could be:

    When I was walking down the road my nose felt cold.

Walking down the road,
my nose felt cold.

- It is important to ensure that the participle is not left hanging on its own. It needs to be clearly attached to the subject of the clause, or reworded.

    Opening the door, a strong smell came to my nostrils.

should be reworded

    Opening the door, I smelt a strong odour.

or

    When I opened the door, a strong smell came to my nostrils.

present tense

The **present tense** of a verb has three main categories.

1 simple present tense

I laugh
he laughs
they laugh

2 present continuous tense

I am laughing
he is laughing
they are laughing

3 present perfect tense

I have laughed
he has laughed
they have laughed

principal / principle

Principal is used mainly as an *adjective*, meaning first in importance.

Wheat was the *principal* crop grown in that area.

It can also be a *noun*.

The *principal* of the high school spoke at the assembly.
She reinvested the *principal* at a lower interest rate.

Principle is always a *noun*, meaning a standard of behaviour or fundamental truth.

They kept to their *principles* and would not be tempted.
If you follow these *principles* you will be successful.

print media (see media, p. 82)

This refers to the media which are produced in print form, such as newspapers, magazines and so on.

prologue

The **prologue** is a *preface* or *introduction* most frequently associated with drama. It was commonly used in Restoration drama in England in the 18th century and in the plays of Ancient Greece. The prologue provided those facts necessary for the audience's understanding of the play and these were announced by a speaker at the beginning. One of the most famous prologues is Chaucer's 'General Prologue' to *The Canterbury Tales*.

In modern terms the word refers to an introduction to any literary work.

pronoun (from *pro,* meaning 'for', 'on behalf of')

The **pronoun** is used in place of a noun. Pronouns are useful shorthand words that avoid the repetition of nouns for people, places and things.

Steve saw the car and then *he* watched *it* drive off.

Without pronouns the sentence would read:

Steve saw the car and then Steve watched the car drive off.

- A pronoun should NOT be used unless there is a noun, or its equivalent, standing for the pronoun.

I hope to become a lawyer because *it* pays well.

The pronoun *it* is not linked to any noun. It should be rewritten as:

I hope to become a lawyer because the profession pays well.

(See also separate listings under **demonstrative, interrogative, personal, possessive, reflexive, relative.**)

propaganda

Propaganda is writing which deliberately promotes a one-sided view in order to gain support for a particular political or social viewpoint or belief. Propaganda has little truth behind it and is rather a crude form of persuasion.

Initially the term was neutral and simply meant the propagation, or spreading of a belief. However, in modern dictatorships it has come to have strong negative connotations. It has been used in mass communication in order to manipulate public opinion solely to serve the purpose of the *propagandist.*

proper nouns

Proper nouns are *capital letter nouns* — names of particular people, places and things, and are written with a capital letter.

> *Perth   Frank   Sydney   Grand Hotel   New Zealand*

If something has a special title, such as Education Committee or Australian Medical Association, it is also treated as a proper noun.

prophecy / phrophesy

Prophecy (pronounced *profesee*) is the noun.

> The congregation believed that the *prophecy* would come true.

Prophesy (pronounced *profesigh*) is the verb.

> There are always some people who claim they can look into the future and *prophesy* events.

prose

The term **prose** is applied to all forms of written or spoken expression which do not have a regular rhythmic pattern. It is most often used to designate conscious, cultivated writing. Interestingly, and unusually, prose in all literatures has developed more slowly than verse.

protagonist   (from the Greek *protos,* meaning 'first' and *agonistes,* meaning 'actor'; pronounced pro-tag-onist)

This term was used for the actor who took the main part in a play. Today we use the word to refer not only to the main character in a play or story, but also the most important person(s) in any particular situation.

When the **protagonist** is in conflict with another important character, that person or rival is referred to as the **antagonist**. Often in a narrative the *hero* is the **protagonist** and the *villain* is the **antagonist.**

proverb

A **proverb** is a short, wise saying. It is a sentence or phrase which briefly and strikingly expresses some recognised truth or shrewd observation about life. The saying is not necessarily meant in the literal sense, but is used figuratively to suggest a warning, or may contain advice. It has been preserved by the oral tradition, but may also derive from written literature.

Proverbs may owe their appeal to the use of different devices. Examples of these are:

● metaphor

> Still waters run deep.

- antithesis

    Man proposes, God disposes.

- a play on words

    Forewarned is forearmed.

- rhyme

    A friend in need is a friend indeed.

publication (see **writing process**, p. 163)

pun

A **pun** is a humorous play on words that is based on the similarity of
sound between two words with different meanings.

    Drinking and driving are a grave mistake.

punctuation

Punctuation is used for the written word so that the reader may gain
meaning. In speech the meaning is conveyed by the use of emphasis
and pauses. Punctuation has to serve the same purpose with written
language, and groups the words into meaningful chunks for the
receiver to process. Without punctuation the meaning may be distorted
and confusing.

    The house was bought this week for $100 000 we can renovate it easily.

This could be:

    The house was bought this week. For $100 000 we can renovate it easily.

or:

    The house was bought this week for $100 000. We can renovate it easily.

My father who is seventy said Denise is losing weight.

This could be:

> *"My father who is seventy," said Denise, "is losing weight."*

or:

> *My father, who is seventy, said, "Denise is losing weight."*

It is important to have the correct punctuation in all written work to help the reader gain the meaning. That is why there are full stops, commas, question marks, exclamation marks, colons, semi-colons, apostrophes, inverted commas. (See separate listings for each of these.)

purple prose / purple patch

These terms refer to a passage of intensely colourful writing which stands out from the rest of the prose around it. Writers sometimes use this technique to create a sudden heightening of rhythm or diction.

The term is frequently used derogatively of writers who have piled up this device in a way that suggests that the text is being 'overworked'.

purpose and audience

Purpose and **audience** refer to *why* and *for whom* communications are formed or framed. They are the consideration given to any oral or written communication; the originator *(sender)* is consciously aware of the aim *(purpose)* of the message and the receiver *(audience)*. This influences the consideration of *style, tone (register), form,* and *structure* when framing the piece.

Q

quatrain

A **quatrain** is a stanza of poetry consisting of four lines that usually have a rhyme pattern of *a b a b,* but which can vary from this pattern.

question mark (from the Latin word *quaere,* meaning 'inquire')

The symbol **?** originated from the first letter of the Latin word *quaere.* It is placed after the words that are actually spoken to indicate that a question has been asked.

> "How are you today?" asked Fiona.
> Gary replied, "Do you really need my help?"

- The question mark is placed inside the inverted commas but is not used if there is not an exact quotation of the actual words spoken.

> I asked him what he intended to do.

- The question mark is not normally needed after a request.

> Will you please forward a copy of the brochure.

quiet / quite

Quiet (pronounced *kwyet*) consists of two syllables. It is usually used as an *adjective* meaning absence of noise.

> We live in a *quiet* street.
> Why don't you keep *quiet*?

It can also be used as a *noun*, meaning without anyone knowing.

> He did it on the *quiet*.

Quite (pronounced *kwite*) consists of one syllable. It is an *adverb* meaning completely or absolutely.

> I've had *quite* enough, thank you!
> You're *quite* right.

quip

A **quip** is a retort or sarcastic jest or any witty saying, particularly a *pun* (see p. 113).

quotation

A **quotation** refers to previously spoken or written words that are repeated. Such quotations or quotes can be copied exactly from another

person's work, but their source must be acknowledged (see **plagiarism,** p. 101). They are indicated by quotation marks, and are used to
- emphasise or reinforce a point
- summarise a point
- justify or support a point about a literary text in analytical essays.

quotation marks / speech marks / inverted commas

These can be single or double and are used for
- titles of short stories, poems, paintings, radio and television programmes, and films (see also **title punctuation,** p. 150)

    'The Man from Snowy River'
- indicating when a word or group of words is quoted from another source

    Julius Caesar is famous for the words 'I came, I saw, I conquered'.
- identifying the use of direct speech

    "What's the time?" he asked.
- indicating a quote within the words spoken, when single quotation marks are used

    "I bet he'll say 'What's the time?' when you ask him to leave," said Anne.

quoting from a text

This is used to support and illustrate a point made, particularly in an essay. The following are useful guidelines to follow:
- Enclose the words in quotation marks.
- Copy the words exactly as used in the original.
- Indicate omissions by ellipses (. . .), which can introduce or end the quote, or occur during the quote.
- Explain the relevance of the quote and how it supports the point(s) being made.
- Limit quotes to three or four lines, and do not over-quote.

    After Mrs Dubose's death, Atticus tells Jem and Scout of her illness and her morphine addiction. The children are then able to understand and sympathise with her displays of bad temper. Atticus tells the children he wanted them 'to see what real courage is, instead of getting the idea that courage is a man with a gun in his hand'. (p. 118)
    Scout realises that the setting of the alarm-clock was used to increase Mrs Dubose's period of tolerance without morphine, '. . . that the alarm-clock went off a few minutes later every day . . . The alarm-clock was the signal for our release'. (p. 115)

    Harper Lee, *To Kill A Mockingbird*

R

raise / rise / raze

Raise is a *transitive verb* meaning to erect or move to a higher position.

> They *raised* a monument to his memory.
> He *raised* the bar above his head.

Rise is an *intransitive verb* with the parts *rose* and *risen*, and means to get up, ascend, mount to a higher position.

> Now's the time to *rise* and shine.
> The sun *rose* at six o'clock that morning.

Rise is also a *noun*, and is commonly used to indicate an increase.

> Mark had a *rise* in salary.
> The *rise* in temperature came unexpectedly.

Raze is a *verb* meaning to demolish, to destroy completely.

> The building was *razed* to the ground.

recur

Recur is a verb that means to happen again, especially at regular intervals. Its forms are *recurs, recurring,* and *recurred.* (There is no word *reoccur.*)

redundancy (see **tautology**, p. 146)

Redundancy occurs most often in expressions such as

- *the reason . . . is because of.* The last part — *is because of* — is redundant to the meaning in such sentences as:

> *The reason* for the higher prices of cars *is because of* increased import duties.

Omit *is because of* and write:

> The reason for the higher prices of cars is increased import duties.

- *is due to/owing to the fact that.* The last part — *the fact that* — is redundant to the meaning in such sentences as:

> The long delay *is due to the fact that* an accident blocked all lanes of traffic.

Omit *the fact that* and write:

> The long delay is due to an accident which blocked all lanes of traffic.

referencing

Referencing is used to help the reader find as easily as possible the resource referred to. It may be:

- *footnotes*, which are references placed at the bottom of the page or at the end of the chapter. These may be highlighted in the text by asterisks, daggers or numbers.

    ' . . . America is ungovernable.' *
    * Conrad, J. *Nostromo*, Penguin, London, 1979, p. 161.

- *bibliography*, which is an alphabetical list of resources placed at the end of the publication (see **bibliography**, p. 19).

The following abbreviations may be found in referencing:

- *ibid.* (*ibidem*), meaning 'in the same place', which is used when a sequence of references come from the same book.

    Prain, V. *Left to Write*, Oxford University Press, Melbourne, 1990, p. 8.
    ibid., p. 51.

- *op. cit.* (*opere citato*) meaning 'in the work cited', which is used when referring to a resource used earlier.

    Prain, *op. cit.*, p. 78.

- *et al.* (*et alii*), meaning 'and other people', which is used when referring to a resource written by a number of people. Only the first author is cited.

    Doughty, P. *et al.*, *Language in Use*, Edward Arnold, London, 1971.

- *passim*, meaning 'throughout', which is used when a reference is scattered throughout pages too numerous to list.

reflective writing

This refers to a form of personal 'real life' writing. It recounts personal experiences, feelings or events from the past, and reconsiders them in relation to the present and future.

reflexive pronouns

Reflexive pronouns reflect or refer to the subject in a clause. They all end in *-self* or *-selves:*

    myself yourself himself itself oneself ourselves yourselves themselves
    Napoleon (**subject**) appointed *himself* as leader and thwarted others (**subject**) who wanted the position for *themselves.*
    Sue (**subject**) was at fault *herself,* but expected that I (**subject**) would incriminate *myself* too.

register (see also **tone**, p.151)

Register is the term used to describe the different types of language and the tones that are used in particular situations and contexts. Language use varies according to

- its purpose and audience
- subject matter
- speaker or writer's relationship with others
- mood of speaker
- written or spoken mode of language.

In other words the intended *audience* and the *purpose* of the communication dictate the **register** in which it will be transmitted.

relative clauses

Relative clauses are introduced by relative pronouns such as *that, which, who* and *whom*.

> The boy, *whom* you saw at the station, is coming this way.
> His friend, *who* lives in Bunbury, is here on holiday.

They are often subordinate adjectival clauses, modifying the noun that they follow.

relative pronouns

Relative pronouns relate or link clauses to the noun to which they refer. Relative pronouns are *who, whom, which, that, whose, who(m)ever, whatever, whichever*.

> The suit *that* he bought last week is with the tailor, *who* is making alterations.

• *that* relates to *the suit; who* relates to *the tailor*

> The books *which* are on the table belong to Mr Brown *whom* I do not know.

• *which* relates to *the books; whom* relates to *Mr Brown*

Points to note:

• Use *who, that, which* for subjects.
• Use *whom, that, which* for objects.
• Use *who* and *whom* for people; *that* and *which* for things.

repetition (in literature)

In literature **repetition** refers to the rhetorical device where word(s) or phrases are repeated to create specific effects. It serves to add emphasis, force and clarity to the text when used deliberately; however, when it is applied carelessly, such as in *tautology* (see p. 146) or *redundancy* (see p. 117), it is unpleasantly noticeable.

It is particularly effective in the art of *persuasion*, and is thus a favourite technique used by orators. In verse it often forms the *refrain* or *chorus*, and appears to be an inescapable element of poetry.

report

A **report** is an account that is based on the research or investigation of a particular topic. Data are collected from various sources and then presented according to the requirements of the report. The steps to follow when preparing to write a report are:

1 Find information or data on the topic.

2 From the data, select the relevant main ideas and supporting detail that the report topic requires.

3 Organise the data into categories under headings.

4 Sequence the categories so that there is a clear link between them.

5 Order reports, under headings and sub-headings, under one of two main referencing systems:

- Roman numerals and lettering

    I MAIN HEADING
      A Sub-heading
        i Detail
      B Sub-heading
        i Detail
        ii Detail

- Decimal notation

    1.0 MAIN HEADING
      1.1 Sub-heading
        1.1.1 Detail
      1.2 Sub-heading
        1.2.1 Detail
        1.2.2 Detail

6 Keep details of your sources of information so that you can provide a bibliography at the end of your report.

reported speech (see indirect speech, p. 67)

Reported speech indicates that the words spoken are not being quoted in their original form but are being reported or recorded. The words being reported are often introduced by *that*.

resolution (in literature) (see also denouement, p. 40)

Resolution is part of the dramatic structure of plays and refers to the rounding-off of the action — the conclusion — of the conflict.

- In *tragedy* the resolution may also be referred to as the *catastrophe* or the final stage in the *falling action*, and can involve the death of the hero or designate an unhappy ending (or event).
- In *comedy* the term used is more likely to be *denouement*, which in French means the 'unravelling', 'untying' or 'unknotting' of the *complication*.
- **Resolution** is also used to refer to the outcome of the climax in a narrative.

résumé / curriculum vitae (see job applications, p. 72)

review

A **review** is a notice of a book (text), play or film. A review announces a work, describes its subject, discusses its method and technical qualities, and examines its merit when compared with other similar works. Its function is to give readers or an audience an accurate idea of the book, play or film under consideration in order that they may decide whether to read or view it.

No headings are used in reviews; they should be written in continuous prose. The main steps to follow in writing a review of a novel are:

REVIEW WRITING PRO FORMA

For a novel
- Give the correct title and author.
- Describe the setting — how significant is it to the story or theme?
- Describe the characters and plot.
- Give more details about the main character(s).
- Comment on style and structure.
- Note to what audience the text is pitched.

If you are reviewing a play, you should also comment on
- its direction
- stagecraft and techniques such as costumes, lighting, music and sound effects.

When reviewing a film, attention should be given to
- camera treatment, that is angles, shots, point of view
- special effects, as well as sound
- symbolic treatment.

---

rhetoric

Rhetoric is the manner of effectively organising spoken material to appeal to the intellect. It is a way of presenting ideas emotionally and imaginatively to impress, persuade or convince.

rhetorical question

A **rhetorical question** is a question that is asked for its rhetorical effect and does not require a reply, nor is it intended to induce a reply. Its main principle is that since its answer is obvious and usually the only one possible, a deeper impression will be made than if the speaker makes a direct statement.

Rhetorical questions are mostly framed to elicit a 'No' response, thereby creating a stronger emotional appeal and involving the audience more directly.

rhyme

Rhyme is the similarity of sound, or the echo effect of sounds, within two or more lines of verse. The sameness of sound is based on both vowels and succeeding consonants. However, rhyme is more than a mere ornament; it affords pleasure through the sense impression it makes, and it serves to unify and distinguish divisions of the poem by establishing the form of the stanza.

There are various types of rhyme:

- **end rhyme**, by far the most common type, which occurs at the ends of lines
- **internal rhyme** (also called *Leonine rhyme*), which occurs at some place after the beginning and before the closing syllables of lines.
- **beginning rhyme**, which occurs in the first syllable (or syllables) of lines.

rhyme scheme

The **rhyme scheme** refers to the pattern, or sequence, in which the rhyme sounds occur in poems. This rhyme pattern is indicated by allocating a different letter of the alphabet for each new rhyme sound that occurs in the verse, that is, the same rhyme sound is given the same letter.

He hangs between his wings outspread	*a*
Level and still	*b*
And bends a narrow golden head	*a*
Scanning the ground to kill	*b*
Yet as he sails and smoothly swings	*c*
Round the hill-side	*d*
He looks as though from his own wings	*c*
He hung down crucified	*d*
Andrew Young, 'The Eagle'	

rhyming couplet (see **couplet**, p. 36)

rhythm (in poetry)

Rhythm in poetry is the movement, or sense of movement, communicated by the rise and fall of the language used, or the arrangement of stressed and unstressed syllables. Certain metrical patterns (see **metre**, p. 82) can be used consciously or deliberately to create particular effects.

RSVP

RSVP is an abbreviation for the French expression *répondez s'il vous plaît*, which means 'reply if it pleases you', or merely 'please reply'. It is usually found at the end of written invitations.

run-on lines (in poetry) (see **enjambement**, p. 49)

run-on sentences (see also **sentence**, p. 126)

Run-on sentences are sentences which try to include too many main ideas. These sentences run on or run away with themselves and become much too cumbersome and difficult to read. They need to be broken down into two or three separate sentences.

> The next job is the car engine, this will cost money and you know I'm strapped for cash at the moment perhaps I'll win Lotto what do you think of that?

should be written:

> The next job is the car engine. This will cost money and at the moment I'm strapped for cash. Perhaps I'll win Lotto. What do you think of that?

S

satire

Satire is a form of writing where the main purpose is to attack some fault, pretension or hypocrisy shown by a person, society or whole nation of people. Its aim is to reveal the abuses and follies that exist and hold them up to ridicule. Some well-known satires are Jonathan Swift's *Gulliver's Travels*, George Orwell's *Animal Farm*, and Evelyn Waugh's *The Loved One*.

A modern example of satire is Bruce Dawe's description of a politician receiving an honorary degree:

> *Was ever man so naked though well-dressed*
> 'Epiphany'

which has overtones of the story of 'The Emperor's New Clothes', itself a satirical comment on human vanity and unwarranted adulation.

Satire can work through *exaggeration*, when the subject is blown up out of all realistic proportions; through *analogy*, when a ridiculous equivalent is substituted for a real-life situation; and through *reversal*, when the whole situation is turned upside-down so that an entirely new perspective is offered for consideration.

scansion

Scansion is the dividing of lines of verse into feet by marking the accents and stress patterns to determine the metre. It provides an indication of how the rhythmical effects in the poem have been attained.

> What is / this life / if full / of care,
> We have / no time / to stand / and stare.

sci-fi / science fiction

Science fiction is the speculative or predictive fiction based on scientific and technological developments and the possible consequences for society. It has evolved as a particular genre because of developments in science and technology in our societies. Ever since the Industrial Revolution, people have been making imaginative predictions of how science and technology could change their lives. These changes would take place on our own planet or on other planets in the universe. It has become a distinct form of fiction writing based on the 'What if...?' of scientific thinking. Alternative worlds, societies and life-styles are being envisaged. Some forecasts made by early Sci-Fi writers such as H. G. Wells and Jules Verne have been fulfilled: humans are able to go to the moon; stay underwater; live in space; and robots are gradually replacing humans in many work situations.

semi-colon

A **semi-colon** is a stronger mark of punctuation than a comma. It is used:

- to separate main clauses in a sentence when the conjunctions *and, but, or* and *for* are omitted

    I walked down the road; I saw my brother.
    Please open the window; the room is getting stuffy.
    You can go; you can stay; just make up your mind.

- to separate main clauses that are connected by *however, nevertheless, consequently, therefore, thus*

    I'd like to buy some; *however*, they're too expensive.
    She said nothing directly; *nevertheless*, I'm sure she meant me.
    Megan's been away; *consequently*, she's missed a lot.

- to separate main clauses that are long and contain commas

    When he was stung he felt a sharp pain in his leg; but as there was no swelling he thought nothing of it.

- to separate items in a long list where commas are used

    Applicants must be neat, well dressed, and speak clearly; have legible handwriting and a good command of written English; and be able to work under pressure for long hours.

sentence (from the Latin word *sententia*, meaning 'a chunk of thought or feeling')

A sentence has:
- a capital letter for the first word
- a full stop, question or exclamation mark at the end
- a subject and a finite verb.

It is a sequence of words that can stand alone to:
- make a statement   *I can see you.*
- ask a question   *Are you happy?*
- give a command   *Stop that.*
- make an exclamation   *What a pity she's away!*

The main kinds of sentences are : complex, compound, loose, periodic, run-on, simple.

(See separate listings for each of these.)

separate

Separate means to break something into *parts,* and it helps to remember this when spelling *s e P A R a T e S.*

Separate gives the words *(in)separable* and *separation.*

serial / cereal (see **cereal**, p. 24)

setting (time [when] and **place** [where])

Setting **refers** to the literal place and time in which the action of a work of fiction occurs, as distinct from the emotional aura — mood and atmosphere (see also *sympathetic setting* under **mood**, p. 84) — evoked by the work. The place may be real, imaginary, fanciful, historical, contemporary or even a combination of these.

sexist language

Sexist language refers to those features or uses of language that are said to be biased against women. The masculine pronouns *he, him* and *his* and expressions such as *man, chairman,* and *mankind* are seen to be reinforcing the stereotype of the dominant male in society.

Ms has been introduced into the language as an alternative to *Miss* and *Mrs* to avoid the distinction in the marital status of women that is not made for men, who are always *Mr.*

Female forms of nouns such as the following are disappearing:

actress   authoress   comedienne   heroine   manageress

More general terms are now used to include both genders. No longer are there:

policemen/women	but	*police officers*
foremen	but	*supervisors*
salesmen/women	but	*salespersons* or *sales consultants*.

As there are no sexless singular words for *he* and *she* or *him* and *her* in formal English, it is often better to re-word a sentence to make it 'sexless'. The following sentence illustrates this point:

Anyone is able to join the club if he or she pays his or her subscription.

This is better worded as:

All who wish to join the club may do so by paying their subscriptions.

Shakespearean / Elizabethan sonnet   (see **sonnet**, p. 130)

shall / will

These words are used
- to express the future

I/we *shall*
you/he/she/it/they *will*
I *shall* be there tomorrow. They *will* be with me.

- to express willingness, a wish, determination, or an intention

We *will* get our way, come what may.

- to give a command

You *will* do as you're told.

short story

A **short story** can be told or read in a brief space of time. Those which are longer are called novels. The short story is one very popular way of telling a story. It:
- is fairly brief
- is usually about a few main characters
- is set in one place at one particular time
- is about a conflict or problem that the characters face
- is based on one main action which solves the problem
- finishes on a climax that leads to a resolution.

SHORT STORY STUDY PRO FORMA

Ask these questions when reading a short story:

Plot (see p. 101)
• What happens? Why?
• To whom does it happen?
• What are the outcomes? Are they possible? Are they credible?
• Is the outcome predictable?
• Is the title significant? Is it ironic or descriptive?
• How does the story end? A surprise ending or punch line?

Setting (see p. 127)
• Is it appropriate?
• Does it help to develop plot and characters? How?
• Are there changes, or just one background?
• Is a particular atmosphere created?
• What effect does it have?

Characters (see p. 24)
• Are they rounded, or flat?
• If they change or develop, consider how.
• What do we learn about them through *actions, speech, appearances, others*?

Conflicts (see p. 33)
• What kinds of conflicts arise?
• Do the conflicts arise out of the setting?
• How do they affect characters?
• Are the conflicts resolved? How?

Theme (see p. 149)
• What is the significance of the events?
• Is there an underlying message?
• What interpretation can be offered about events?

Point of view (see p. 104)
• Who tells the story?
• How does this affect our understanding of the story?

should / would

These are tenses of the verbs *shall/will*.
• **Should** is usually used to mean *be obliged to*.
• **Would** is usually used to mean *wish, resolve, be determined to*.

I *should* have done it.	meaning	*I ought to have done it.*
I *wouldn't* do it.	meaning	*I didn't wish to do it.*
I *would* point out . . .	meaning	*I wish to point out . . .*

simile

A **simile** is a figure of speech in which two things are compared and one is said to be *similar* to the other. The words 'like' or 'as' are used to introduce a simile. It is a literary device used to make language more colourful and imaginative.

The cloud of smoke hung over the houses *like some giant black umbrella*.

simple sentence

A **simple sentence** consists of one main clause that expresses one complete thought.

He (**subject**) bought (**finite verb**) a present for his mother.

A simple sentence can be just one word.

Stop!
(*You* = **the understood subject;** *stop* = **finite verb**)

All main clauses can stand as simple sentences when the rest of the sentence is removed.

singular

The **singular** of a noun or pronoun refers to a single person or thing.

SINGULAR NOUN	SINGULAR PRONOUN
a book	it
the boy	he
a woman	she

slang

Slang is language that is not generally acceptable as standard English. It does not have a particular subject base, such as jargon. What is slang today may later become acceptable, but some becomes unfashionable and does not survive.

She's very *trendy*; look at her *gear*!

soliloquy

A **soliloquy** is a dramatic convention where a character speaks his or her thoughts aloud, apparently unheard by others who may be on stage.

sonnet

A **sonnet** is a strongly-patterned form of poetry that originated from the song lyric, and was developed in Italy during the Renaissance. It is referred to as the classical **Petrarchan sonnet** after Petrarch the Italian poet. It was introduced into England during the 16th century when Shakespeare made it a popular form, and is known as either the **Elizabethan** or **Shakespearean sonnet**. Its popularity has been sustained through to modern times.

Early sonnets dealt mainly with love, whereas present day sonnets are usually an expression of strong personal feeling and emotion.

All sonnets have fourteen lines and use the *iambic rhythm* (light/heavy stress) as the main metre form, usually *iambic pentameter* (five feet to each line). There are a variety of sonnet forms and these are usually distinguished by different rhyme schemes.

CLASSICAL OR PETRARCHAN SONNET

Rhyme scheme   *Alternative line arrangements*

— a
— b
— b
— a   Two quatrains which express the poet's motive and first thoughts on the topic
— a
— b
— b
— a

Block of 14 lines

Octave of 8 lines

Quatrain of 4 lines

Quatrain of 4 lines

→ Volta, or turning point →   Volta   Volta

— c
— d
— e   Sestet which expresses the poet's second thought sequence
— c
— d
— e

Sestet of 6 lines

Sestet of 6 lines

ELIZABETHAN OR SHAKESPEAREAN SONNET

Rhyme scheme   *Alternative line arrangements*

— a
— b
— a
— b

— c
— d   Three quatrains
— c
— d

— e
— f
— e
— f

Block of 14 lines

Three quatrains of 12 lines

Quatrain of 4 lines

Quatrain of 4 lines

Quatrain of 4 lines

— g   Concluding couplet
— g

Couplet of 2 lines

Couplet of 2 lines

speech marks (see **quotation marks**, p. 116)

spelling (see also **spelling rules**, p. 133)

Spelling is important so that a reader can process the communication as quickly and easily as possible.

The following are some commonly misspelt words:

accommodation	*gauge*	*queue*
accidentally	*humorous*	*rhythm*
acquire	*jewellery*	*seize*
argument	*library*	*sincerely*
benefited	*maintenance*	*successful*
calendar	*necessary*	*surprise*
definitely	*occasion*	*weird*
embarrass	*parallel*	*woollen*

If any of these prove difficult, try spelling them on paper. It is better to have a word to look at rather than try to spell it aloud. Use the LOOK, SAY, COVER, SAY, WRITE, CHECK strategy to help remember. This means:
- look and write correctly
- say aloud several times, exaggerating pronunciation
- cover, and say again, trying to visualise the word
- write
- uncover and check
- repeat if incorrect.

spelling rules

Spelling rules do exist to a certain extent, although words in English seem to follow patterns more than submit completely to rules. Some general guidelines are as follows:

1 ie and ei words

The *i before e except after c* applies to nearly all words in which the vowel sound is *ee*.

● *i before e*

belief brief chief hygiene niece relieve

● *e before i*

ceiling receive perceive deceive conceive

Exceptions are:

caffeine counterfeit either foreign heinous
forfeit neither protein seize weird

Points to note:

● When the vowel sound is *ay*, then *ei* is used.

beige neighbour reign sleigh veil weigh.

● *Leisure* is pronounced like *pleasure*.

2 Adding a suffix

● If the word ends in a single consonant, has only a one-vowel syllable, and the suffix begins with a vowel, then the last letter is usually doubled.

ship ship*ped* ship*ping*
drum drum*mer* drum*ming*

Exceptions are the letters *w, x, y*, which are never doubled.

box box*er* box*ing*
row row*ed* row*ing*
stay stay*ed* stay*ing*

Points to note:

● When words have a two-vowel syllable, they do not double the last letter.

boat boat*ing*
heat heat*ing*
cook cook*ing*

● If the word has more than one syllable, has the stress on the final syllable, ends with a single vowel and a consonant, then double the last letter.

begin begin*ning*
prefer prefer*red*

admit   admit*tance*
occur   occur*rence*

Exceptions are:

transfer*able*   prefer*able*   picnick*ed*

• If the word has two or more syllables, ends in a single consonant, has a single vowel before the last letter, or has the stress on the first syllable, then usually the last letter is not doubled.

open	open*ing*	open*er*
benefit	benefit*ing*	benefit*ed*
gossip	gossip*ing*	gossip*er*
carpet	carpet*ing*	carpet*ed*

Exceptions are:

worshi*pped*   kidna*pped*   forma*tted*

• If the word ends in the letter *l*, has a single vowel before the letter *l*, and has the stress on any syllable, then usually the last letter *l* is doubled.

travel	travel*ling*	travel*ler*
compel	compel*ling*	compel*led*
rebel	rebel*ling*	rebel*lion*

Exceptions are:

unparallel*ed*   parallel*ogram*   capital*ism*   natural*ist*

• If the word ends in a consonant and the letter *y*, and has the suffix *-ing* added, then usually there is no change to the word.

try	try*ing*
worry	worry*ing*
fly	fly*ing*
terrify	terrify*ing*

• If the word ends in a consonant and the letter *y*, and has a suffix other than *-ing* added, then *y* changes to *i*.

happy	happ*iness*
beauty	beaut*iful*
busy	bus*iness*
mercy	merc*iless*

Exceptions are:

dryness   shyness   slyness

• If the word ends in a single *l* and *e*, and has the suffix *-ly* added, then usually there is no change.

nice*ly*   complete*ly*   accidental*ly*   definite*ly*   ora*lly*

Exceptions are:

duly   truly   wholly

3 -or or -our

- If the word is referring to a person, *-or* is usually found.

  actor   counsellor   visitor   conductor   director

- If the word is an abstract noun, *-our* is usually found.

  colour   favour   humour   honour   vigour
  valour   vapour   labour   behaviour

- When the suffixes *-ation, -ous, -ise,* and *-ific* are added to *-our* words, then the *u* is dropped.

  coloration   humorous   honorific   vaporise   vigorous

- But *-our* is kept when adding *-able, -er, -ite, -ful, -less, -ist.*

  colourless   favourite   behaviourist   honourable   labourer

4 -ise or -ize

- There are some verbs which are never spelt *-ize,* but always *-ise.*

  advertise   advise   compromise   despise   devise   exercise
  improvise   revise   supervise   surprise   televise

- Words which must end in *-ize* are:

  assize   capsize   prize   size

- The *-ise* suffix is used more often now than *-ize,* for example:

  recognise   criticise   nationalise   civilise

Instead of the ending *-ize,* it would therefore be better to reserve the *-ize* ending for only the four words listed above.

5 -able or -ible

There is no definite way to decide on the correct ending, but the following may help:

● More words use the living form -*able* than -*ible*.

● If the opposite of the word starts with *un-*, it is likely to end in -*able*.

● If the word starts with *il-*, *in-*, or *ir-*, it is likely to end in -*ible*.

Exceptions are:

capable/incapable	intelligible/unintelligible
separable/inseparable	probable/improbable
excusable/inexcusable	

Point to note:

● -*able* is always *probable*, while -*ible* is only *possible!*

6 -ance, -ence or -ent

● There is no definite way to decide on the correct ending, but the following may help:

-*able* often changes to -*ance*
　　allowable/allowance

-*ant* always changes to -*ance*
　　dominant/dominance

-*ible* often changes to -*ence*
　　intelligible/intelligence

-*ent* always changes to -*ence*
　　prominent/prominence

Exceptions are:
　　preferable/preference, resistible/resistance

7 -ary or -ery

● There is no definite way to decide on the correct ending, but the following may help:

-*ary* is more often an adjective than a noun
　　imaginary temporary necessary contrary stationary

-*ary* is often a noun that describes a person rather than a thing
　　missionary actuary secretary

-*ery* is more often a noun than an adjective
　　stationery confectionery distillery

-*ery* is often a noun that describes a thing rather than a person
　　bakery machinery cemetery

8 -ede or eed

- Most verbs end in -*ede*.

  accede concede intercede recede stampede supersede

- There are three verbs which end in -*eed*.

  succeed exceed proceed

split infinitive

A **split infinitive** occurs when an adverb or adverbial phrase is placed between *to* and the base form of the verb which make the infinitive.

INFINITIVE	SPLIT INFINITIVE
to run	to slowly run
to collapse	to quickly collapse
to protest	to strongly protest
to complete	to without further delay complete

It would be better to avoid the split infinitive by writing:

to run slowly

to collapse quickly

to protest strongly

to complete without further delay

- There are times when the split infinitive is inappropriate, such as:

  They were told *to loudly shout* when the villain appeared.

would be better worded:

They were told *to shout loudly* when the villain appeared.

and

He tried *to with much patience explain* the problem.

would be better worded:

He tried *with much patience to explain* the problem.

spondee

Spondee is a metric foot that consists of two stressed syllables only. It is not a pattern that is maintained throughout a stanza, but occurs most frequently at the beginning of a line.

> Milton! thou shouldst be living at this hour.
> Wordsworth, 'To Milton'

stanza

A **stanza** is a group of lines in poetry that form the basic structure of the poem. Most poets do not vary the stanza structure once it is established and keep to this division. The pattern of the stanza is determined by the number of lines, the number of metrical feet in each line, and the rhyme scheme. A majority of poems have four-line stanzas.

The number of lines to a stanza determines its type: *couplet*, two; *tercet*, three; *quatrain*, four; *quintet*, five; *sestet*, six; *septet*, seven; *octave*, eight.

stationary / stationery

These words are often confused.

Stationary is an adjective meaning 'not moving', 'standing still', 'stopping in one place'.

> The cars in all three lanes were *stationary* after the accident on the bridge.

It helps to remember the *-ary* ending by noting the *a* in st*a*nd, or by rhyming *-ary* with *tarry*, which means to remain in one place.

Stationery is a noun meaning 'writing materials', such as pens, paper, pencils, envelopes, and so on.

> The requests for *stationery* were being cut back drastically to reduce office costs.

It helps to remember the *-ery* ending by noting that the word **stationery** comes from *stationer*, and that the words pens, pencils, and *e*nvelopes all have an *e*.

stereotype (from the Greek *stereo*, meaning 'solid, three-dimensional' and *typos*, meaning 'image or type')

The term **stereotype** was used originally to refer to a printing plate that had been cast in metal from a mould. The word is now mainly used to mean a standard way of representing a particular kind of person. The term 'stock character' is sometimes used because such characters are stock images of a group of people who can be either loved or hated according to the preconceived ideas of the reader or viewer. Value judgements are made, often unconsciously, and stereotyped characters meet with either approval or disapproval. Prejudices may be reinforced and the stereotype's worth evaluated according to how well he or she represents a group.

Television series and serials, pressured for time and controlled by a restricted budget, often need to present characters who can be recognised easily and who are representative of a particular group, such as doctors, lawyers, politicians, housewives, teenagers, policemen, and migrants. Stereotype characters are exploited freely because they are quickly categorised and their role in the narrative is easily understood.

That's it Meryl, break the stereotype.

storey / story

Storey is the level or floor of a building.

> We live on the second *storey* of the apartment building.
> They were constructing a thirty-*storey* block of offices.
> She parked in a multi-*storey* carpark.

The plural of **storey** is **storeys.**

Story is a tale, a narrative.

> He is a good *story-teller*.
> That's a tall *story*.

The plural of **story** is **stories.**

stream of consciousness (see **point of view**, p. 104)

style

Style refers to the way individual writers choose words to construct sentences and paragraphs that reflect their unique way of using language for a specific purpose and effect.

To achieve their objectives and make their stories more effective, writers consider, among other things, the following points of style:

POINT OF VIEW	first or third person
FORM OF NARRATION	diary
	letters
	narrative prose
	flashback
VOCABULARY	choice of words
	how words are used
SYNTAX	sentence structure
	sentence length
	punctuation
DEVICES/TECHNIQUES	repetition
	imagery
	symbol
	tone

subject

The **subject** of a sentence or a clause is the word, or group of words, that performs the action of the verb. To locate the subject, find the verb and ask *who* or *what* is performing the action described by the verb.

The *boy* (**subject**) ate (**verb**) the apple.
The *two old friends* (**subject**) met (**verb**) in the supermarket.
The *accident* (**subject**) happened (**verb**) very quickly.
Has the *car* (**subject**) gone (**verb**)?

- A *singular* subject needs a *singular* verb.
- A *plural* subject needs a *plural* verb.

(See **subject/verb agreement**.)

subject / verb agreement

This means choosing the correct form of the verb to agree with the subject.

- A *singular* subject will have a *singular* verb.

  The boy (**singular subject**) *has eaten* (**singular verb**) the apple.

- A *plural* subject will have a *plural* verb.

  The boys (**plural subject**) *have eaten* (**plural verb**) the apples.

- A subject can consist of noun(s), word(s) used as noun(s), or pronoun(s).

  If *he, she* or *it* can be used for the subject, then the subject is singular.

  The packet of biscuits (**singular subject**) *is* (**singular verb**) not in the cupboard.

  If *they, you* or *we* can be used for the subject, then the subject is plural.

  The packets of biscuits (**plural subject**) *are* (**plural verb**) not in the cupboard.

Points to note:

- The conjunction *and* is usually a good indicator of a plural subject.

  She *and* her friends *are* going on holiday.
  Do my mother *and* sister *look* alike?

- If the conjunction *and* is not used, but words such as *with, in addition to, as well as, together with*, or *including* are used, then the verb agrees with the first subject.

  His friend, *as well as* his parents, *was* going to be there.
  My bicycle, *including* the saddle-bags, *has* been stolen.

- A relative pronoun (*who, which, that*) may be singular or plural depending upon the word(s) to which it refers. If the word(s) is singular, then the verb following the relative pronoun is singular.

  She found *the coat* (**singular subject**) which *was* (**singular verb**) in the wardrobe.

- If the word(s) is plural, then the verb following the relative pronoun is plural.

  > He is one of *those people* (**plural subject**) who *are* (**plural verb**) always late.
  > He found *the tea and milk* (**plural subject**) that *were* (**plural verb**) in the pantry.

- A collective noun usually takes a singular verb.

  > *Our class* (**collective noun**) *works* (**singular verb**) quietly, sometimes.

- Titles of books, plays, films, paintings and songs take a singular verb.

  > *Pride and Prejudice was* written by Jane Austen.
  > *Cats is* a superb musical.

- Nouns which are in a plural form but have a singular meaning take a singular verb.

  > *Mathematics* (**plural noun**) *is* (**singular verb**) a terrible subject for me.
  > *Aerobics* (**plural noun**) *is* (**singular verb**) a popular keep-fit pastime.
  > *The news* (**plural noun**) on television *is* (**singular verb**) being jazzed up to become 'info-tainment'.

- Subject noun phrases agree with the verb, not the complement which comes after the verb.

  > *One of Sydney's main features* (**singular subject noun phrase**) *is* (**verb**) the Botanical Gardens (**complement**).
  > *A few days away on holiday* (**plural subject noun phrase**) *are* (**verb**) a pleasant break (**complement**).

- If the two parts of the subject refer to a single person or thing, the subject is singular.

  > *His friend and colleague* (**singular subject**), Mr Brown, *was* (**singular verb**) helping him.
  > *His car and only transport* (**singular subject**), a Holden, *is* (**singular verb**) in for repair.

His friend and colleague, Mr Brown, was helping him.

subjunctive

The **subjunctive** is one of the four moods of the verb. Its function is to indicate a wish, a condition, or a purpose. It is usually found in sentences that state *if* and *that*.

> I suggest *that* this *be* done immediately.
> *If* I *were* you, I would go.
> It is recommended *that* he *be* given leave.
> Far *be* it for me to suggest otherwise.

subordinate / dependent clause

The **subordinate** (or **dependent**) **clause** is a clause that cannot stand on its own but depends on a *main* or *independent* clause to complete its meaning.

> *When he reached the top of the hill* (**subordinate clause**), he sat down with relief (**main clause**).

A subordinate clause can do the work of an adjective, an adverb or a noun.

sub-plot

A **sub-plot** is a minor complication running through a story or play which tends to parallel the main plot. This secondary plot interest, if handled skilfully, contributes to the main plot. Writers use sub-plot(s) to create intricacies and surprises in their stories or plays.

suffix

A **suffix** is an element attached to the end of a word to form a new word. Suffixes are used in four main ways:

1 to change a word from one part of speech to another

adjective to noun	happy + *ness*	happi*ness*
adjective to adverb	quick + *ly*	quick*ly*
adjective to verb	smart + *en*	smart*en*
noun to adjective	boy + *ish*	boy*ish*
verb to noun	agree + *ment*	agree*ment*
verb to adjective	prefer + *able*	prefer*able*

2 to show how a noun changes from singular to plural

> cat cat*s*   church church*es*   tomato tomato*es*

3 to show how an adjective changes to form a comparison

> small small*er* small*est*   big big*ger* big*gest*

4 to show how a verb changes its form

> laugh laugh*ed* laugh*ing*   stop stop*ped* stop*ping*

summary

A **summary** is a piece of writing reduced to fewer words than the original by keeping only the essential information while retaining the meaning of the original. The following steps should be taken when summarising:

- Skim read to find out what the passage is all about.
- Note the main ideas and supporting detail for each paragraph.
- Use notes to write a first draft.
- Edit the draft, reorganise where necessary.
- Check to see that all main points are included.
- Ensure that the summary reads smoothly, retains meaning, and is less than one-third of the original.

superlative adjective (see comparative/superlative, p. 29)

superlative adverbs (see comparative/superlative, p. 29)

suspense (in literature)

In literature **suspense** refers to the anxiety and anticipation that are created when the reader is unsure of what will happen next. Writers often use *stepping stones of suspense* as a major device for securing and maintaining the reader's interest. The suspense element may be either of two main types:

1 the outcome is uncertain and the suspense lies in the question of *who* or *what* or *how*.
2 the outcome is inevitable from the events which have gone before and the suspense resides in the reader's anticipation of exactly *when*.

syllable

A **syllable** is the basic unit of pronunciation. It consists of a vowel or a vowel sound with either a consonant before or after it, or sometimes both.

through	thr*ou*gh	(one syllable)
rhyme	rh*y*me	(one syllable)
chaos	ch*a*+*os*	(two syllables)
open	*o*+p*en*	(two syllables)
humorous	h*u*+m*or*+*ous*	(three syllables)
receiving	r*e*+c*eiv*+*ing*	(three syllables)

symbol

A **symbol** is used when a writer wishes to attach a particular meaning to an object, person or situation. It represents something that the writer wishes us to note and gain meaning from. The albatross in 'The Rime of the Ancient Mariner' has become a symbol for a cross that has to be borne.

synonym

A **synonym** is a word which means the same as another word.

close   *near*
observe   *watch*
shut   *closed*

synopsis

The **synopsis** is a summary or a condensation of the main points of a literary work, such as a play or a novel.

syntax

Syntax refers to the rules that govern the ways in which words are organised in phrases, clauses and sentences to make meaning. The following words need to be rearranged to make meaning:

jumped John high fence the

becomes

John jumped the high fence.

Sentence structure is usually

SUBJECT   +   VERB   +   OBJECT
John (**subject**)   *jumped* (**verb**)   *the high fence* (**object**)

T

tautology

Tautology refers to saying the same thing twice, but using different words. Many tautologies become established expressions, for example:

free gift
I personally
join together
I saw with my own eyes
repeat again
final conclusion
new innovation

Many, like the following, should be avoided whenever possible.

There was *intermittent rain* followed by *occasional showers*.
He found an *empty house* that was *uninhabited*.
A *dead corpse* was lying at the bottom of the stairs.
She made an *attempt to try* to avoid the collision.

tense (of verbs) (from a Latin word meaning 'time')

The **verb tense** is the form of the verb which indicates when something happened: *present, past* or *future*. The changes that a verb makes are called *inflexions*. Every verb has four principal parts which are used as a basis for forming tenses.

PRESENT	PRESENT PARTICIPLE	PAST	PAST PARTICIPLE
run	running	ran	run
sing	singing	sang	sung
swim	swimming	swam	swum
walk	walking	walked	walked
listen	listening	listened	listened
see	seeing	saw	seen

From these the various *present, past* and *future* tenses are formed.

PRESENT FORMS	PAST FORMS	FUTURE FORMS
he runs	he has run	he will run
she is walking	she had walked	she will have walked
we see	we have seen	we shall see
I am swimming	I had been swimming	I shall have been swimming
they are singing	they sang	they will be singing

Note: The future tense is formed by adding 'will' or 'shall' to present and past participles. Other tense changes are formed by using the verbs 'be' or 'have' with the present and past participles.

tetrameter (from the Greek words *tetra,* meaning 'four' and *meter,* meaning 'measure')

Tetrameter refers to a line of poetry that consists of four metrical feet, and also a stanza composed of such lines.

Tetrameter occurs in the first and third lines of this stanza:

> *They made / a pact / between / them both, /*   (TETRAMETER)
> They made it firm and sure,
> *That who / soe'er / should speak / the first. /*   (TETRAMETER)
> Should rise and bar the door.
>> Anonymous, 'Get up and Bar the Door'.

than

When **than** is followed by noun(s)/pronoun(s) only, it indicates an incomplete clause where the verb has been omitted. This can create confusion, such as in:

> I like David more *than Sam.*

This sentence can mean two different things:

> I like David more *than Sam does.*
> I like David more *than I like Sam.*

This confusion needs to be avoided by ensuring that either the clause is given in full or the correct pronoun is used. The following sentence is another example of such confusion:

> She likes her dog better *than him*.

Which meaning is intended?

> She likes her dog better *than she likes him?*
> She likes her dog better *than he does?*

The writer must decide and state clearly what meaning is intended.

Completing the *than clause* also avoids pronoun errors where the forms *me, him, her, us, them* are incorrectly used.

> Tony is taller *than he* (is).   NOT *him*
> She is cleverer *than I* (am).   NOT *me*
> We paid more *than they* (did).   NOT *them*

the

This is the most frequently used word in the English language. It is called the *definite article*, and can be pronounced *thee* before vowels such as

> apple   elephant   orange

but is frequently shortened to *th-* before

> butter   water   car

and other nouns starting with a consonant.

For emphasis, as in the expression 'Are you *the* John Clarke?', *the* is again pronounced *thee*.

their / they're / there

These words become confused because they have a similar pronunciation.

Their is the possessive form meaning belonging to them.

> He visited *their* home last week.
> *Their* holiday is coming to an end.

They're is the contraction of *they are*.

> *They're* staying with us over the weekend.
> I wonder where *they're* hiding the presents.

There denotes a place and can be linked in its spelling with the other word for place: *(t)here*.

> If you look over *there*, you might find it.
> *There* is no room left in the restaurant.

Here is a sentence with all three:

> I wonder if *they're there* on *their* bicycles.

theme

The **theme** is the central idea or comment on some important issue that lies behind the events in a story, play or poem. A writer's purpose and the structure of the story, play or poem are closely linked. Together they provide the thematic content, thus giving the reader food for thought.

there is / there are

The contraction **there's** is inclined to disguise the difference between **there is** and **there are.**

There's is short for **there is** and should go before a noun in the singular.

There is someone (**singular**) outside waiting to see you.
There is no time (**singular**) to do that now.

There are should be used before a plural.

There are two ways (**plural**) to do this job.
I hope that *there are opportunities* (**plural**) to relax next week.

It is important to note the plural in longer sentences.

There are your aunt in Sydney and your uncle in Brisbane to be considered.

Point to note:

There, as well as *here,* is not a subject. The verb in these sentences is agreeing with the singular or plural subject that follows it.

third person point of view (see **point of view**, p. 104)

three unities

These refer to the importance of *action, time,* and *place* as the principles of dramatic structure. These were proposed by the Greek, Aristotle, who lived in the period 300 years BC. It was said that the action should last no longer than twenty-four hours, and that there should be only one setting. Many playwrights ignored these requirements, including Shakespeare. Many modern dramatists are less concerned with the tradition of the three unities than the total emotional effect of their work.

title punctuation

This term refers to the accepted ways of punctuating a variety of titles when the piece is handwritten. There are two conventions, depending on the type of work referred to.

1 Underline

novels	To Kill a Mockingbird
poetry anthologies	Progress of Poetry
films	Breaker Morant
plays	Romeo and Juliet
long poems	Rime of the Ancient Mariner
newspapers	Sydney Morning Herald
periodicals/magazines	Cosmopolitan

2 Use inverted commas for

chapters	'The Woman Pays'
essays	'Why I am Pale'
poems	'The Highwayman'
short stories	'His First Flight'
radio/TV programmes	'Sixty Minutes'

to / too / two

These are called homophones, but each performs in a different way.

To is a *preposition* and functions in that way in sentences such as:

He climbed *to* the top of the hill.
She enjoyed telling stories *to* children.

Too is an *adverb* which means *as well as, in addition to, extremely,* or *more than.*

He is *too* young to be invited.
I hope that you can come, *too.*

Two is a *noun* and stands for the number 2.

> Here are *two* tickets for the show.
> *Two* is company; three's a crowd.

This sentence uses all three words:

> When you get *to* the supermarket, buy *two* packets of pet food because the cat is hungry, *too*.

tone

Tone is the attitude that writers take towards the subject and the reader. In the same way as speakers may adopt a friendly, pompous, serious, comic, condescending or provocative tone of voice towards their topic and the audience, so writers adopt similar approaches to their readers. The tone of the writing is influenced by the literary devices used, and these will combine to create a mood for the reader. The writer *implies the tone,* and the reader *infers the mood.* In all communications, **tone** is created by the transmitter and *mood* is created by the receiver.

The following extracts are descriptions of places. As the writers describe the places, so their attitudes towards them are revealed.

> For example, nobody could seriously deny that the most beautiful of all cities is Venice: the Shakespeare of cities, as it was once called, all on its own, water-lapped, shadow-dappled, tower crowned, gilded and flagged and marvellously chimneyed, stacked so subtly beside its lagoon that as you sail past its palaces in your long black gondola its layers seem to be moving, building behind building like a marble ballet.
>
> Jan Morris, 'A Passion for Cities'

> It [Coketown] was a town of red brick, or of brick that would have been red if the smoke and ashes had allowed it; but, as matters stood it was a town of unnatural red and black like the painted face of a savage. It was a town of machinery and tall chimneys, out of which interminable serpents of smoke trailed themselves for ever and ever, and never got uncoiled. It had a black canal in it, and a river that ran purple with ill-smelling dye, and vast piles of building full of windows where there was a rattling and a trembling all day long, and where the piston of the steam-engine worked monotonously up and down, like the head of an elephant in a state of melancholy madness.
>
> Charles Dickens, *Hard Times*

The language chosen by each writer conveys the tone. Thus the tone of the first extract might be described as *enthusiastic, warm, adulatory.* We sense that the writer's attitude is positive; she approves and praises Venice. The tone of the second extract, however, might be described as *gloomy, depressing* and *condemnatory.* We sense that the writer's attitude is negative; he disapproves of and dislikes Coketown.

> **STRATEGIES TO DETERMINE TONE**
>
> Ask these questions:
> - What is the writer's purpose or intention?
> - Is the stance taken by the writer *positive, negative, neutral, formal, informal?*
> - Do some words and expressions have strong connotations?
> - Is the language colourful and descriptive?
> - Do the images reflect the writer's attitude to the subject?

topic sentence (see **main idea**, p. 81, and **paragraph**, p. 94)

tragedy

Tragedy is the term used in drama for depicting the events that occur to a person who, because of shortcomings or flaws in his or her character, finally faces some catastrophic or disastrous outcome. The greater the person, the more acute is the tragedy; or, the higher they rise, the harder they fall.

The purpose of **Greek tragedy** was to arouse the emotions of pity and fear and, in this way, produce in the audience a catharsis or purging of these emotions. In other words, the Greeks had a good cry and then went home which, for some people today, is the main reason for seeing some films.

In **Shakespearean tragedy** (written during a period of monarchy) the protagonists were mainly kings and rulers. These people, whose actions affected many, often contributed to their own downfall because of some tragic flaw in their characters, and the conflicts they faced. The tension was built towards eventual disaster by the protagonists' inability to control the forces at work, and frequently resulted in their insanity and collapse. Ghosts, apparitions, graveyards, witches and other supernatural effects were common, all contributing to the murder and mayhem that preceded the resolution.

The **modern tragedy** expresses and reflects what is happening in a society at a particular time, and it is the grief, misery and disaster which face the ordinary person that concern many present day playwrights. Today, people are often portrayed as the victims of social, hereditary and environmental forces.

tragic flaw

Tragic flaw is the weakness or defect in character that leads to the downfall of the hero in a tragedy. It is not necessarily a vice or depravity that constitutes the flaw, but it may be caused by bad judgement, some inherited weakness, or an unwillingness to listen to advice. Once this is expressed in action and decision, the character is doomed. Hamlet, Lear, Othello and Oedipus are famous examples whose tragic ends were brought about by 'the great error or frailty', as Aristotle called it.

tragic irony

Tragic irony is the contrasting of an individual's hopes and dreams with what is finally and realistically achieved. The early years of ambitions and ideas lead to later frustrations and finally death.

King Lear's rejection of his daughter, Cordelia, the one who loves him most, is an example of tragic irony.

The poem 'Death the Leveller' points to the tragic irony of what awaits all of us.

> Sceptre and Crown
> Must tumble down
> And in the dust be equal made
> With the poor crooked scythe and spade.
> > James Shirley

transactional writing

Transactional writing is writing that sets out to *transact* — to negotiate, conduct business arrangements, reach decisions, and achieve goals in a formal way. The transactional function is a means to an end, and it takes its form mainly in report, note, summary and formal letter writing. It is language being used to get things done by informing, requesting and persuading.

transitive verbs

Transitive verbs are verbs that take a direct object. They are the opposite to *intransitive verbs* (see p. 70), which take no direct object.

> He *bought* a bicycle (**direct object**) last week.
> On her way to school, Kath *met* her friend (**direct object**).
> Seeing the dog, they *shut* the gate (**direct object**).

In these sentences, *bought, met,* and *shut* act as transitive verbs.

trimeter (from the Greek words *tri*, meaning 'three' and *meter*, meaning 'measure')

Trimeter is used to describe a line or stanza in a poem that consists of three metrical feet. These are usually *iambic*.

Trimeter occurs in the second and fourth lines of this stanza.

> They had not sailed a league, a league,
> A league, / but bare / ly three, /   (trimeter)
> When the sky grew dark, the wind blew loud,
> And an / gry grew / the sea. /   (trimeter)
>   Coleridge, 'The Rime of the Ancient Mariner'

trochee

Trochee is a metric foot in poetry that consists of two syllables, the first one stressed and the second one unstressed. It is indicated by /∪. It is the reverse of the *iambic foot* (∪/). The trochaic foot occurs in

> Comrades, / leave me / here a / little /
> While as yet 'tis early morn:
> Leave me here, and when you want me,
> Sound upon the bugle-horn.
>   Tennyson, 'Locksley Hall'

U

uninterested / disinterested

These two words do not mean the same thing; they are not synonyms.

Uninterested, with the prefix *un*, meaning *not*, means not interested, indifferent, bored, not wanting to know about.

> He was *uninterested* in the cricket and wished they'd stop watching it.

Disinterested, with the prefix *dis*, meaning *apart from*, *detached*, means free from interest in, unbiased, impartial, no self-interest, without involvement.

> As she was a *disinterested* observer, she was able to offer an objective assessment of the dispute.

As she was a disinterested observer, she was able to offer an objective assessment of the dispute.

unique (from the Latin word *unus*, meaning 'one')

The word **unique** is an adjective which means 'the only one of its kind'.

This is a *unique* painting.
His car is *unique*.

If something is the *only one of its kind*, then it cannot be qualified in any way, and words such as *rather, quite, less, very, absolutely, more, most* should not be used with the word **unique**. Something is either unique or it is not. There are no gradations.

unities (see **three unities**, p. 150)

until / till

These words are interchangeable, although **until** is generally used for starting a sentence.

Until you are listening, I shall not continue.

There are no such words as *'til* or *'till* in English.

usage / use

Usage (pronounced *you-sidge* or *you-zidge*) is a noun that means the way in which something is used, employed, treated, and how this becomes established through custom and practice.

Expressions are: *language usage, contemporary usage, rough usage, careful usage.*

Use can be a noun (pronounced *yous*) or a verb (pronounced *youz*) that means the *act of using* or *state of being used*.

I have no *use* for the article. (**noun**)
The machine has broken through constant *use*. (**noun**)
Do you have any *use* for this? (**noun**)
She *uses* her brains to succeed. (**verb**)
I think they just *use* people. (**verb**)

V

values and attitudes

Values are the ideas, beliefs, interests and convictions that a person or a group of people accept as the appropriate standards for conducting their lives. Such values as friendship, wealth, family life or popularity influence the ways in which people behave.

Attitudes are particular opinions or views that a person or a group of people adopt towards a set of values. A group of people may agree on a particular value and accept its ideas and beliefs (such as a religious or political conviction), but their attitudes may differ and opinions on how to achieve the values will conflict. Attitudes are differing individual reactions to a value.

Since all people hold cultural values and attitudes, these are present in all visual and verbal communications. Cultural influences are inescapable. Visual values and attitudes can be readily identified in a medium such as advertising, where consumers are being urged to buy a product, adopt a lifestyle, and take up an attitude. The advertisers are covertly conveying the message that these values can be embraced by purchasing the product.

The values and attitudes conveyed in a verbal communication are not always as obvious. The language being used has to be examined closely. The ideological position being taken by the transmitter is more deeply embedded in the communication. The language symbols are the only guide, and the following need to be noted:

- *characters* how presented
- *setting* its links with characters and conflicts
- *conflicts* underlying values and attitudes presented
- *emotions* connotations and associations that are being highlighted
- *audience* group targeted, values and attitudes that are being reinforced
- *structure* forms of presentation and narration, along with imagery created and references made, that underpin and support the values and attitudes being promoted.

Whether viewing or reading a text, the audience is encouraged to share a particular set of values and beliefs. Often the audience is being influenced to accept the values as the only correct ones to follow as these relate to gender, race, religion, and general lifestyle. What is important to note is that the mass media are promoting values and attitudes continually. There is no value-free mass media communication. News, documentaries, sports and current affairs are all value and attitude 'loaded', relying heavily on subtleties of language, the use of heroes, villains, victims, stereotypes, conflicts, actions and resolutions to achieve their intentions.

verbal irony

Verbal irony occurs when a writer or speaker implies an understanding that is different from the obvious meaning of the original wording. The intention may be humorous or even an outright attack on the topic, and this lies behind what is said.

Newspaper headlines may be ironic in their intention, such as:

> Minister of Police arrested for dangerous driving.
> Swimming instructor rescued by surf lifesavers.

Verbal irony is often used by satirists, and George Orwell in *Animal Farm* exploits this in one of the animals' seven commandments:

> *All animals are equal but some animals are more equal than others.*

Napoleon and the pigs, who are in charge and supposedly working for the good of all, have given themselves complete freedom to do as they like in a society that is supposed to offer equality to all animals. The whole novel is an ironic comment on communist Russia.

verbs

In their finite form **verbs** are the essential ingredient in all sentences. If there is no *finite verb* (see also p. 56), then there is no sentence. Their function is to express action, events, or to refer to existence.

ACTION   John *kicked* the ball into the goal.
EVENT   The show *ended* at ten o'clock.
EXISTENCE   Her friend *was* a police-officer.

Kicked, ended and *was* are all finite verbs.

Was is the past tense of the verb *to be* which, together with *to become*, is a linking verb which shows the existence or relationship between the subject and the noun(s) following the verb.

Other verb forms are: *active/passive, auxiliary, finite, gerund, infinitive, mood, tense, transitive/intransitive, subject/verb agreement.*
(See separate listings for each of these.)

verbosity

Verbosity refers to the use of more words than are needed. The tendencies are:

● adjective over-use

true facts	*terrible tragedy*
grave emergency	*unfilled vacancy*
definite decision	*fatal death*

● adverb over-use

certainly sure	*definitely dangerous*
finally concluded	*very obvious*

● prepositional phrases

with the exception of	*inasmuch as*
in excess of	*for the reason that*

● verb expansion

I am of the opinion that
I am informing you that
I am in communication with

Verbosity can be described as *padding,* a technique often used in government offices and such woolly wording as:

The opportunity is taken to mention that you may pay by instalments, but *it should be pointed out very clearly and completely that in the current climate* no further credit can be given until the account has been paid.

The words in italics are merely *padding* and could be omitted without loss of meaning.

verb phrase

The **verb phrase** is a verb linked with an auxiliary verb which together expresses *time* or *passive voice*.

He *must visit* (**verb phrase**) his mother soon.   (TIME)
They *would have taken* (**verb phrase**) longer without him.   (TIME)
The doors *were locked* (**verb phrase**) on the outside.   (PASSIVE VOICE)

vernacular

Vernacular is the commonly spoken language of a particular people or place.

verse

Verse has two main meanings:
1 a line of poetry
2 a particular form of writing that depends upon rhyme, rhythm and a stanza structure to achieve its effect.

via (the Latin word meaning 'way')

The term **via** acts as a preposition and is pronounced *vy-er*. It is used in such sentences as:

Come to Australia *via* (by way of) Singapore.
Send it back *via* (by way or means of) the courier.

volta (see **sonnet**, p. 130)

Volta is the change in thought or feeling that separates the octave from the sestet in a classical or Petrarchan sonnet.

vowel

A **vowel** is the sound represented by any of the letters *a, e, i, o, u*. These are open sounds, with the lips and teeth being open to pronounce them. Other letters are *consonants*, requiring the use of lips, teeth or tongue for pronouncing. The consonant *y* may serve as a vowel in such words as *rhythm* or *rhyme*.

weather / wether / whether

These words are pronounced the same, which leads to some confusion.

Weather can function as a *noun, adjective* or *verb*.

NOUN	We are having atrocious *weather* at the moment.
ADJECTIVE	The *weather* side of the boat took the gale-force winds.
VERB	The roof had *weathered* badly and required painting.

Wether is a noun, meaning a castrated ram.

The *wethers* were sold for a good price at the market.

Whether is a *subordinating conjunction* which often implies doubt or choice and can be replaced with *if*.

I wonder *whether* (if) he will succeed.
I have no idea *whether* (if) they will come.

who / whom

Who is used when it is the *subject* of a verb.

Who (**subject**) will come (**verb**) with me?
The man *who* (**subject**) came (**verb**) yesterday is back.
They are people *who* (**subject**) are (**verb**) always late.

Whom is used when it is the *object* of a verb.

The boy *whom* (**object**) you saw (**verb**) is outside.
Whom (**object**) did you see (**verb**) yesterday?
He is one of the people *whom* (**object**) I know (**verb**).

It helps to determine whether to put **who** or **whom** by asking if:

- **who** can take the place of *he, she* or *they*.

I know (*he, she, they?*) will win.

therefore:

I know *who* will win.

- **whom** can take the place of *him, her* or *them*.

I met my friend (*him, her, them?*) I'd not seen for ages.

therefore:

I met my friend *whom* I'd not seen for ages.

As all prepositions take an object, *whom* should be used after such words as *to, from, by, with* and *for*, in exactly the same way as *to me, from us, by them, with her* and *for him*.

whose / who's

Whose is a *possessive*, meaning *of whom* or *to whom* does something belong, and also *of which* or *to which* does something belong.

> *Whose* book is that?
>
> The rainbow, *whose* colours were so dominant, arched across the sky.
>
> I told them *whose* fault it was.
>
> The car, *whose* windows were broken, was towed away.

Who's is a *contraction* of *who is*.

> I wonder *who's* (who is) going to be there.
>
> Can you tell them *who's* (who is) going to win?

Can You tell them who's going to win?

will / shall (see **shall**, p. 128)

writing

See separate listings for **descriptive, emotive, expressive, factual, narrative, persuasive, transactional.**

writing process

The **writing process** refers to the stages that writers go through as they proceed from their first thoughts to their final product. The writing process helps us to take full advantage of our ideas and experiences so that we can write more interestingly for our audience. Like any other learning process, we need to go through a number of stages before success is achieved. The three main stages are: *drafting, editing, publication.*

1 *Drafting*
This is the hardest stage, when the writer
- considers audience, purpose, and form
- sets ideas down for the first time
- writes freely on the topic
- concentrates on meaning and an appropriate style
- produces a rough copy that indicates the direction the writing will take.

2 *Editing*
This is the important middle stage, when the writer
- looks critically at the draft copy
- adds, deletes, rewords, elaborates and revises first thoughts
- corrects spelling, punctuation and grammatical structure
- checks to note how *audience, purpose* and *form* are combining to set the tone and achieve an effective result
- considers illustrations, diagrams and charts for possible inclusion
- refers to objective readers for guidance or help.

3 *Publication*
This is the final stage, when the writer
- provides the final copy for the reader
- adds professional touches to the presentation
- offers neatly handwritten, typed or word-processed copy
- presents work in appropriate copy form — booklet, report, review, etc.
- evaluates responses made by readers.

Y

your / you're

Your is a *possessive adjective* that means 'belonging to you'.

Here is *your* book.
Your mother is waiting for you.

You're is a *contraction* for *you are*.

You're (you are) just in time.
I think *you're* (you are) in luck because *you're* (you are) holding the winning ticket.

I think you're in luck because you're holding the winning ticket.